Rain of Ruin

Also by the Authors

The Way It Was. Pearl Harbor: The Original Photographs (1991)

D-Day Normandy: The Story and Photographs (1993)

"Nuts!": The Battle of the Bulge (1994)

By Donald M. Goldstein and Katherine V. Dillon

The Williwaw War (1992)

The Pearl Harbor Papers: Inside the Japanese Plans (1993)

(with Gordon W. Prange)

At Dawn We Slept: The Untold Story of Pearl Harbor (1981)

Miracle at Midway (1982)

Target Tokyo: The Story of the Sorge Spy Ring (1984)

Pearl Harbor: The Verdict of History (1987)

December 7, 1941: The Day the Japanese Attacked Pearl Harbor (1988)

God's Samurai: Lead Pilot at Pearl Harbor (1990)

(with Masataka Chihaya)

Fading Victory: The Diary of Admiral Matome Ugaki (1991)

By J. Michael Wenger and Robert J. Cressman

Steady Nerves and Stout Hearts: The Enterprise *(CV-6) Air Group at Pearl Harbor, 7 December 1941* (1989)

Infamous Day: The Marines at Pearl Harbor, 7 December 1941 (1992)

Rain of Ruin

A Photographic History
of Hiroshima and Nagasaki

DONALD M. GOLDSTEIN, KATHERINE V. DILLON,

and J. MICHAEL WENGER

BRASSEY'S
WASHINGTON   LONDON

LIBRARY OF CONGRESS CATALOGING-IN-PUBLICATION DATA

Goldstein, Donald M.
    Rain of ruin: a photographic history of Hiroshima and Nagasaki/
Donald M. Goldstein, Katherine V. Dillon, and J. Michael Wenger.
      p.   cm.
    Includes bibliographical references and index.
    ISBN 1-57488-033-0
    1. Hiroshima-shi (Japan)—History—Bombardment, 1945—Pictorial
works. 2. Nagasaki-shi (Japan—History—Bombardment, 1945—
Pictorial works.   I. Dillon, Katherine V.   II. Wenger, J. Michael.
III. Title.
D767.25. H6G65   1995
940.54′25—dc20   95–2164

Designed by Robert Freese

10 9 8 7 6 5 4 3 2 1

Printed in the United States of America

Contents

Preface

The idea for this book came to Goldstein when he led a group of undergraduate students from the University of Pittsburgh's Semester-at-Sea program on a field trip to Hiroshima. During this experience, the following thoughts struck him forcibly:

First, Japanese history books contain very little about World War II, its origins and progress. Such subjects are usually glossed over in a page or two. One gains the impression that modern Japanese history begins with the atomic bomb. Of course, that event was devastating, and quite naturally the Japanese tend to stress the horrors while leaving conveniently vague the chain of events that brought it on. As one of the Japanese participants at the Pearl Harbor Conference of December 1991 remarked, the Japanese have not faced up to the truth about the Pacific war, and the story should be told. Lately they have begun to take a more realistic view, making reparations to Korea and admitting to the Rape of Nanking.

Second, many of the American students who have crossed Goldstein's path over the years are almost as ignorant as their Japanese counterparts concerning World War II. Standard American textbooks tend to give short coverage to wars, apparently preferring to concentrate on political, social, and economic events. As a result, these students, lacking a solid frame of reference, tend to accept unquestioningly the thesis that the bomb should never have been dropped.

This is the fourth book in a series by this team depicting key events of World War II, telling the story in photographs. The first three concerned Pearl Harbor, D-Day in Europe, and the Battle of the Bulge.

In this latest book we attempt to present the story of the atomic bombings of Hiroshima and Nagasaki briefly, clearly, and with a minimum of technicalities. The book is divided into eight chapters, as follows:

Chapter 1, "America Builds the Bomb," covers the decision to develop atomic energy and attempt to construct a bomb. In it one meets a number of people involved in the project, both civilian and military. With research well under way, the 509th Composite Group was organized, began training, and established itself on Tinian Island. Germany surrendered, but Japan fought on.

The title of Chapter 2, "Plans and Preparations," is self-explanatory. It follows the course of the 509th's training missions and considers strategy for a possible invasion of Japan. The atomic bomb test is successful, and the 509th moves into an operational phase. The Potsdam Declaration is issued, and Japan officially ignores it. Truman authorizes the atomic bomb mission. The cruiser *Indianapolis* delivers components to Tinian and is later sunk.

Chapter 3, "Target Number One." Final briefings are held, and secrecy lifted as takeoff events and personnel are photographed for history. Seven B-29s participate, with Colonel Paul W. Tibbets piloting the strike aircraft, *Enola Gay*. If weather permitted, destination would be Hiroshima. The chapter tells something of Hiroshima's history, the city's important place in Japan's military establishment, and its exceeding vulnerability to fire.

Chapter 4, "The Hiroshima Bomb," concerns the actual bombing of Hiroshima and portrays much of the devastation. This chapter also describes the initial reaction of the Japanese military and the reluctance to admit that this had really been an atomic bomb (something the Japanese had tried, but failed, to develop). Army and navy investigators confirmed that the bomb had indeed been atomic, and the Emperor ordered his foreign minister to end the war.

Chapter 5, "The Nagasaki Bomb," describes the second atomic bombing, which targeted Kokura; however, visibility was not favorable and the mission, headed by Major Charles W. Sweeney in *Bock's Car*, proceeded to the alternate target, Nagasaki. We tell something of the history and the geography of Nagasaki, the home of two of Japan's largest war plants. This chapter includes many photographs depicting the damage.

Chapter 6, "Peace!" covers the political activities in Japan for and against surrender. Despite two atomic bombings and the Soviet Union's declaration of war, the ultramilitarist faction refused to yield. They argued that Japan had not yet lost the war, and that if the Americans attempted an invasion their losses would be prohibitive. While a majority of the cabinet favored peace, the decision had to be unanimous. Pockets of opposition remained, and not until the Imperial broadcast of August 15 did resistance cease. Japanese were dazed and sorrowful. In contrast, the United States erupted in joy that the war was over.

Chapter 7, "Surrender!" tells of the arrangements for Japan's disarmament and formal surrender, the arrival of the battleship *Missouri* in Tokyo Bay, and the subsequent surrender ceremony.

Chapter 8, "Aftermath," describes the beginning of the Occupation, the suffering that followed the atomic bombings, and the rebuilding of Hiroshima and Nagasaki.

The book is not footnoted, but we have included a brief bibliography of sources we found helpful. Also included is a chronology of the major events leading up to the bombings and Japan's surrender.

We should like to dedicate this book to the hope that the first atomic bombings may be the last.

DONALD M. GOLDSTEIN, Ph.D.
Professor of Public and International Affairs
University of Pittsburgh
Pittsburgh, Pennsylvania

KATHERINE V. DILLON
C.W.O., USAF (Ret.)
Arlington, Virginia

J. MICHAEL WENGER, M.A.
Raleigh, North Carolina

Acknowledgments

We wish to acknowledge with gratitude the help of many whose cooperation was essential to this volume. These include Max Brandt and Phil Williams, who supported us on the project in Japan; Bill Hendricks and Carl Wikman, for their photography and video help; Tom Odegaard, who helped arrange the Hiroshima trip; David MacIssac, who did much of the research at Maxwell Air Force Base; Colonel Richard Rauschkolb, Commander, Air Force Historical Research Agency at Maxwell Air Force Base; Joe Caver, for his research and help in obtaining pictures from the files at the Air Force Historical Research Agency; Robert J. Cressman of the Contemporary History Branch, Naval Research Center, who located many key documents and photographs; Patterson Anthony; Ralph D. Curry (radio operator, *The Great Artiste*); Dr. Mark Griffith and John Lundstrom of the Milwaukee Public Museum, who furnished ideas, records, materials and information; Charles Haberlein, Curator Branch, and Curtiss Utz, Contemporary History Branch, Naval Historical Center; at National Archives, Ruth Dix, who handled photograph orders, and Barry Zerby, who assisted with U.S. Navy records; Brian Nikla of the National Air and Space Museum, who assisted in photo research; at the Suitland Records Center, Gibson Bill Smith, who located critical Navy records relating to the surrender ceremony, and Lieutenant Colonel David Stanley, who assisted in last-minute research at Suitland; Jen Bosworth, Anita Tilford, and Kendall Stanley of the University of Pittsburgh's Graduate School of Public and International Affairs, for their help with the manuscript; Barb Runett, for help in clarifying some of the pictures from Hiroshima; Franklin Margiotta, Carsten Fries, Don McKeon, and Kelley Meagher of Brassey's; and last, Tallan Price Tubbs-Talley, for his research and gathering of photographs.

Introduction

In looking back at any historical event, the temptation exists to view it through the prism of the present. This can be interesting, but is hardly helpful. The past must be seen in its own light, or comprehension is impossible. Nowhere is this more true than in the case of the atomic bomb. One cannot understand the decision to use it unless one examines briefly the alternatives as they appeared to the participants at the time.

To all intents and purposes Japan had been defeated for months; however, the problem was not to defeat Japan but to secure her surrender—a very different proposition. Quite simply, the Japanese did not believe in surrender. Their nation had never lost a war. Moreover, her fighting men were indoctrinated with the concept that surrender was not an option. So deeply ingrained was this notion that even after two atomic bombs and the entry of the Soviet Union into the war, the Japanese military establishment continued to oppose capitulation bitterly.

Aside from the atomic bombs, the Allies—the United States in particular—had two major options. First, they could rely upon maritime blockade plus stepped-up B-29 raids and naval bombardment to force Japan's surrender. Even if this strategy had worked, which is questionable, it would have been no improvement over the atomic solution in terms of devastation. It is important to remember that just one B-29 raid over Tokyo, on the night of March 9–10, 1945, had killed over 100,000 people. If nightly raids had killed only half that number, in a single month 1,500,000 Japanese would have died, not to mention the material destruction.

As for a full-scale invasion, both sides took this prospect with the utmost seriousness. Operation Olympic, the invasion of Kyushu, and Operation Coronet, the invasion of Honshu, were planned to start on November 1, 1945, and March 1, 1946, respectively. No one could predict the ultimate U.S. losses, but the Americans esti-

mated that they could total about a million. They knew better than to underestimate the courage, skill, and tenacity of Japan's military. Fighting in defense of their homeland, they would be truly formidable. More than a million soldiers were stationed in Japan for home defense, their strength including crack combat units pulled out of China and Manchuria.

To counter such an invasion, the Japanese had prepared Ketsu Go No. 6, and many high-level officers had faith that it could succeed. Major General Masakazu Amano, chief of the operations section at Imperial General Headquarters, remarked after the war:

> We were absolutely sure of victory. It was the first and the only battle in which the main strength of the air, land and sea forces were to be joined. The geographical advantages of the homeland were to be utilized to the highest degree, the enemy was to be crushed, and we were confident that the battle would prove to be the turning point in political maneuvering.

The Japanese estimated they could destroy approximately half the invading force offshore, mainly by kamikaze action. The Japanese planners knew that the United States had the manpower and equipment to launch attack wave after attack wave, but hoped the Americans would weary of the slaughter and offer Japan fairly favorable terms. Throughout the war, the Japanese had clung to the delusion that the Americans lacked the tenacity to fight to the end. The landing on Kyushu would have been only the preamble to many battles which, judging from such actions on Okinawa and Iwo Jima, would have been indescribably fierce and bloody. Total casualties and sheer destructiveness would have far exceeded those of the two atomic bombs.

The numbers of those killed in the atomic bombings are at best educated guesses. In August 1978, the Hiroshima Peace Memorial Museum wrote that accurate figures for civilian casualties were still not available. As of March 1995, the exact number remained unknown. At the time of the attack, the Japanese had estimated the casualties at Hiroshima as 71,379 dead or missing, and 68,023 injured, of whom 19,691 were seriously hurt. The United States Strategic Bombing Survey (USSBS) figured the dead at between 60,000 and 80,000, with about the same number of injured. Of the 24,158 Japanese soldiers stationed at Hiroshima, 6,769 were killed. But many civilian residents of Hiroshima died later from the effects of radiation. By August 10, 1946, the research section of the Hiroshima city hall had raised the count to 118,661 dead, 3,677 missing, 30,524 seriously wounded, and 48,606 slightly wounded.

At Nagasaki, the Japanese estimated immediate casualties as 23,753 killed, 1,927 missing, and 23,245 injured. The United States Strategic Bombing Survey (USSBS), which considered these figures low because the Japanese counted only verified cases, estimated 35,000 dead, 5,000 missing, and 60,000 wounded. By later calculations, both estimates were too low. The 1984 *World Book* cited 40,000 killed or missing and a like number wounded, while the 1994 *Encyclopedia Americana* claimed the attack killed 73,884.

Even if one accepts the highest of these figures, then doubles the sum to cover an estimate of related later deaths, the total is still much less than that expected as a result of invasion.

Another "what if" must be considered. Had the war continued, the Allies would have had to accept the Soviet Union as a full partner. Almost certainly Japan would have been divided into two main zones, delaying her recovery by decades, and she would have been very lucky indeed to keep the Imperial dynasty and her way of life.

All told, we cannot escape the conclusion that the atomic bombs saved Japanese lives as well as American.

None of which lessens the fact that the atomic bomb was a fearsome weapon and that humanity would no doubt be considerably happier had it never been invented. At the time, hope was expressed that the bomb's very horror might frighten mankind into recognizing that war was no longer a viable alternative. In his post-surrender broadcast to the nation, General of the Army Douglas MacArthur warned, "Even the lesson of victory itself brings with it profound concern, both for our future security, and the survival of civilization. . . . The utter destructiveness of war now blots out this alternative. We have had our last chance."

The nations have been chastened to this extent: The atomic bomb was never used again. But those who remember the immediate post–World War II period will never forget the pervasive uneasiness that ranged from, at the top, a very real fear for the planet itself down to, at popular level, a spate of science fiction movies featuring various monsters supposedly the products of atomic energy. Gradually it became evident that no responsible nation had any intention of starting a nuclear war. The fear that remained—and remains to this day—is that all too many groups and individuals are irresponsible, and no more to be trusted with atomic energy than a toddler with a box of matches.

MacArthur was overoptimistic in hoping mankind would recognize that war was no longer a sane option. Since World War II, lesser conflicts have followed with monotonous regularity. "It is well that war is so terrible, or we should get too fond of it" is an oft-quoted remark of Robert E. Lee. Indeed, the most cursory reading of any history leads to the dismaying conclusion that humanity must indeed be fond of war, resorting to it at any provocation. This is the real root of the problem, not the atomic bomb as such. All the weapons of war are evil. Those killed at Hiroshima and Nagasaki were no more dead than the victims of conventional weapons.

A fighting man's view of the atomic bomb came from Captain Mitsuo Fuchida, who had led the air attack on Pearl Harbor and who had been one of those investigating Hiroshima the day after the disaster. He felt no resentment toward the United States for dropping the bomb. In his opinion, once a nation embarked upon war, it was obligated to go all out. To possess a weapon that could ensure victory and not use it would be to break faith with that nation's people. Fuchida added that the Japanese had tried to develop the atomic bomb, and if they had succeeded would certainly have dropped it.

It is possible to pity the victims of the atomic bombs without attempting to rewrite history, as the Smithsonian Institution recently attempted. The projected script for an exhibit pertaining to the atomic bombings contained these two astounding sentences: "For most Americans . . . it was a war of vengeance. For most Japanese it was a war to defend their unique culture against Western imperialism." From this sample, one can well imagine the type of exhibit that would have emerged.

This mind-set should not have surprised anyone, because over several years a number of Smithsonian exhibits had displayed a similar anti–United States bias. Such presentations raised relatively little fuss because the exhibit subjects had been somewhat remote in time. However, with the atomic bomb project, the Smithsonian miscalculated. Too many people were still alive who remembered and cared, too many who had had direct experience of some of the less lovable aspects of Japan's "unique culture" to swallow whole the concept of the Japanese as innocent victims of vengeful Americans and "Western imperialism," that hoary chestnut of Japanese wartime propaganda.

As a result of sharp protests from veterans' groups, members of Congress, and John Q. Public, the Smithsonian eventually canceled the exhibit as it had been originally planned.

There is no reason why compassionate Americans should not sympathize with the victims of the Hiroshima and Nagasaki bombs. It is equally appropriate, however, to sympathize with the victims of the Rape of Nanking, where the Chinese estimate Japanese troops killed 300,000—and which the Japanese have only recently admitted ever happened. Nor should we forget the Bataan Death March, or the infamous Japanese prisoner-of-war camps, where starvation and torture were commonplace and where "medical" experiments were conducted fully as horrifying as anything Hitler's goons practiced. Especially, kindhearted Americans should remember Manila, where from February 3 to March 3, 1945, Japanese troops went on a rampage of murder, torture, rape, and general destructiveness all the more sickening because there was no shadow of strategic reason for such action.

The U.S. Army estimated that some 100,000 civilians died during that month—roughly one out of ten Manilans.

We take no pleasure in recalling such atrocities, but it is well that Americans take a balanced view of World War II in the Pacific, despite the wails of the "politically correct." It is equally well to remember that the atomic bomb was not exclusively an American idea. Both Germany and Japan were trying to perfect it, and it would be ludicrous to suggest that either Nazi Germany or expansionist Japan would not have used it. The unhappy fact is that virtually every technological advance has somehow or other been put to military purposes. And there is no reason to hope that this will not continue to be so, with results no one can predict. The clear alternative to a continuing "rain of ruin" is peace. It may be an impossible dream—but humanity had better try.

Rain of Ruin

CHAPTER 1

America Builds the Bomb

Serious consideration of an atomic bomb began for the United States through a chain of European scientists. In 1934, Enrico Fermi of Italy had experimented with bombarding uranium metal with neutrons. Four years later, two German scientists, Otto Hahn and Fritz Strassmann, repeated Fermi's experiment, concluding that the uranium nucleus had indeed split, releasing part of its energy. They passed the word to Lise Meitner—a courageous action, Hitler having exiled her because she was a Jew. In turn, Meitner notified Niels Bohr, a Danish physicist. Much interested, he called for further experiments.

In January 1939, Bohr came to the United States, where he heard indirectly from Meitner that further experiments had confirmed the theory. Bohr carried the word to Princeton's Institute for Advanced Study. World War II began that September, and the prospect of such potentially awesome power in the hands of Adolf Hitler was enough to give nightmares to even the most cool-headed of scientists.

Thus it came about that in October 1939, a friend of President Franklin D. Roosevelt, Alexander Sachs, who had close ties with the scientific community, brought the president a letter from Albert Einstein (1–1). He outlined the situation, including these exceedingly significant words:

> It may become possible to set up a nuclear chain reaction in a large mass of uranium, by which vast amounts of power and large quantities of new radium-like elements would be generated. . . . It is conceivable—though much less certain—that extremely powerful bombs of a new type may thus be constructed.

1–1 Dr. Albert Einstein.

Roosevelt (1–2) did not seem to quite grasp the overriding importance of Einstein's letter. But the next day, Sachs asked him to imagine the result if Napoleon had taken up Robert Fulton's offer to build a fleet of steamboats to cross the English Channel. The navy-minded President got the message.

1-2 President Franklin D. Roosevelt (center), with Stalin (left) and Churchill (right) at the Yalta Conference during early February 1945.

1-3 Dr. Vannevar Bush.

1-4 Dr. John B. Conant, president of Harvard University.

Soon he selected a committee to check out the possibilities, headed by Lyman Briggs, with Commander Gilbert Hoover and Colonel Keith Adamson as members. This committee soon blended with the Office of Scientific Research and Development under Dr. Vannevar Bush (1–3). A list of some of the figures involved reads like a *Who's Who* of academia— John B. Conant (1–4), president of Harvard University; Leo Szilard of Hungary; Karl Compton (1–5), president of the Massachusetts Institute of Technology, and his brother, Arthur (1–6), who headed the physics department of the University of Chicago; Fermi (1–7), who might be said to have started it all; and others of similar caliber.

Meanwhile, the British had been laying the groundwork upon which the Americans would build. The New Zealand–born Baron Ernest Rutherford of Nelson, 1908 Nobel Prize winner in chemistry, had envisioned the energy of the atom as far back as 1902. His pupil James Chadwick discovered the neutron and won the Nobel Prize for physics in 1935. Such findings, with Hahn's discovery of fission action, gave the British a commanding lead.

Thus it came about that on October 1, 1941, Bush could advise Roosevelt and Vice President Henry A. Wallace that British physicists were quite sure that they knew approximately how much uranium would be required to produce a bomb. Whereupon the president agreed to proceed with the project. He could finance it through secret funds.

1-5 Dr. Karl Compton (third from left) at the first meeting of the War
Resources Board on August 17, 1939. Other members are, seated (l-r): Dr.
Harold S. Moulton, acting secretary of the Navy; Charles Edison; board
chairman Edward R. Stettinius; and Assistant Secretary of the Navy Louis
Johnson. Standing: Commander Anton B. Anderson, USN; Admiral Harold R.
Stark, USN; Compton; John L. Pratt; General George C. Marshall, USA; and
Colonel Harry K. Rutherford, USA.

1-6 Dr. Arthur Compton.

1-7 Dr. Ernest O. Lawrence (left), Dr. Enrico Fermi (center), and
Isidor I. Rabi.

1-8 Henry L. Stimson, secretary of war, was directly responsible to the president for the entire atomic bomb undertaking.

1-9 Major General Leslie R. Groves, in executive charge of the Manhattan Project.

To anticipate a bit, the British continued to lead the field until 1943, at which time the realities of the war caught up with them. The atomic bomb promised to be a devastating weapon, but they needed to expand and refine their radar defenses right then and there. So such top physicists as Sir John D. Cockcroft and Mark Oliphant were removed from the field of atomic energy and put to work on radar. The gaseous diffusion plant at Billingham was virtually shut down. Britain sent seventy-five physicists to the United States to cooperate with their American colleagues, passing the torch to the United States which, of course, had been working hard in the atomic energy field and was ready to take over.

In November 1941, Roosevelt named Secretary of War Henry L. Stimson (1–8) to a committee to advise him on nuclear fission. From that time on, this veteran statesman would oversee the project and would prove a rock of strength, fending off inquisitive members of Congress and overeager labor organizers.

Less than a month later, the United States was in the war, and the Manhattan Project had begun, with Major General Leslie Groves (1–9) in charge of the enormous building program inherent in the project.

Three major research and production sites were selected. At Los Alamos, near Alamogordo, New Mexico, the actual weapon would be designed. In charge was Julius Robert Oppenheimer (1–10)—a controversial choice, because in his youth he had been involved in pro-Communist activities. But Groves insisted that Oppenheimer was essential. (Photos 1–11, 1–12, and 1–13 give some idea of the isolation and security consciousness of this post.)

The object was to produce a powerfully explosive bomb by means of reactions among atomic nuclei. The

1-10 Dr. J. Robert Oppenheimer.

1-11 The rear entrance to the Alamogordo, New Mexico, test site during July 1945. Note watchtower at left.

1-13 Main camp at Alamogordo.

1-12 A lonely MP stands watch in one of the watchtowers at the test site.

bombs destined to be used over Hiroshima and Nagasaki would use fission reaction. In the first type, the nuclei of the heavy element uranium-235 split into two lighter nuclei. The fission of one pound of U-235 would equal that of 8,000 tons of TNT.

For this to occur, the U-235 nucleus must pick up a neutron. The nucleus breaks into two nuclei, which frees two or three neutrons, producing further fission reaction. A critical mass of fissile material can produce a chain reaction. If the mass is supercritical, the neutrons increase rapidly. Thus a supercritical mass might explode prematurely or melt. So each component of the bomb must be smaller than the critical mass, i.e., subcritical. For the bomb to be effective, the subcritical must become super-

critical very rapidly indeed. In the "gun-type" bomb used at Hiroshima, a conventional explosive propelled one subcritical mass through a gun-barrellike arrangement into another subcritical mass at the other end.

Obviously to turn theory into reality would require all the brainpower, expertise, technology, and funds the United States could pour into the project.

At Oak Ridge, Tennessee (1–14), the locals could only wonder what was going on in the huge new buildings where hundreds labored without, apparently, producing anything. Actually, they were separating U-235 from U-238, the main isotope in natural uranium. (The shoulder patch worn by personnel of the Manhattan Engineering staff at Oak Ridge is shown in photo 1–15.) The third

1-14 Oak Ridge, Tennessee, seen from the "Oliver Spring" Gate. An anonymous observer said of this entrance to the facility: "The first view the visitor has of Oak Ridge itself . . . (is) not very impressive, but that's the way it was."

1-15 Shoulder patch worn by personnel of the Manhattan Engineering District.

1-16 The Hanford, Washington, facility.

facility, at Hanford, Washington, was busy producing plutonium, an artificial element, from uranium (1–16).

The Nagasaki bomb would use plutonium. The method of fission was the same as for uranium, but the method of detonation was different. The subcritical mass was compressed to become supercritical. In this method, the fissile material was placed in the center of a spherical casing of conventional explosives termed a tamper. When these were set off, an implosion compressed the fissile mass, making it supercritical.

The determined interest in the Hanford facility of members of the Truman Committee to investigate mili-

tary expenditures caused Stimson to cross swords with the then-senator Harry S. Truman—and win (1–17). The earlier discovery, at Berkeley, California, of plutonium freed the project from dependence upon the scarce U-235 and allowed manufacture of an atomic bomb in time to serve its purpose. By December 1942, a workable atomic pile had been established at the University of Chicago, under Fermi's supervision (1–18, 1–19, and 1–20). A truly formidable group of scientists worked with Fermi, and in the future the University of Chicago would be closely associated with nuclear energy in the public mind (1–21).

1-17 President Harry S. Truman speaks at the White House on April 17, 1945, five days following the death of President Roosevelt.

1-18 The University of Chicago's Physics Building.

1-19 The Argonne Laboratory, a research facility near Chicago for the Metallurgical Project.

1-20 The University of Chicago's New Chemistry Building, a part of the Metallurgical Laboratory.

1-21 Scientific Group at the University of Chicago. Front (l-r): Enrico Fermi, Walter Zinn, Albert Wattenberg, Herbert Anderson. Center: Harold Agnes, William Sturm, Harold Lichtenberger, Leona Marshall, Leo Szilard. Back: Norman Hilberry, Samuel Allison, Thomas Brill, Robert Nobles, Warren Nyer, Marvin Wilkening.

1-22 Wendover Field in 1941; Tibbets selected this site in Utah as the training base for the 509th Composite Group. Before its assignment to the 509th, the 393rd Bombardment Squadron trained at Fairmont Field, Nebraska.

1-23 Colonel Paul W. Tibbets, Jr., commanding officer, 509th Composite Group, upon his promotion to full colonel. Note the cardboard eagles on his shoulders.

Groves was now free to pursue the military portion of the project, entitled Operation Silver Plate. By the latter part of September 1944, picked men began arriving at Wendover Field, Utah (1–22)—as miserable a location as could have been found in the United States. However, Lieutenant Colonel Paul W. Tibbets, Jr. (1–23), who chose it from among three possible sites, believed it the best for security purposes; in addition, it had sturdy runways and suitable base facilities.

Tibbets had an excellent record in the European and North African theaters as a B-17 pilot. Early in 1943, he had been ordered to Alamogordo, New Mexico, where he tested the capabilities of the new B-29 bomber (1–24). He had about a year and a half to familiarize himself thoroughly with the Superfortress, when he was summoned to Colorado Springs to meet with Major General Uzal Ent, in command of the Second Air Force (1–25). Tibbets also met Dr. Norman Ramsey, a bomb specialist, and Navy captain William Parsons (1–26), Oppenheimer's chief of weapons development. An intelligent man, Tibbets knew enough about atomic theory to understand what they were talking about, although the idea of an atomic bomb left him surprised and even skeptical.

Ent explained that Tibbets would establish and command a special air group to deliver the bomb. His task was daunting, quite aside from its purely operational aspects. Security at Wendover could not have been tighter. Tibbets could put nothing on paper and would give all reports orally. Normal items could come through normal channels, but if he needed anything out of the ordinary, he was to contact a certain officer at Army Air Force headquarters, using the code name Silver Plate. General

1-24 Two Boeing B-29s on Saipan stand poised for takeoff on the first Tokyo raid of the bombing offensive against Japan, November 24, 1944. Note the tail-gun position of the aircraft at right.

1-25 Major General Uzal Ent, Second Air Force.

1-26 Captain William S. Parsons, senior weaponeer, on loan to the 509th Composite Group from the U.S. Navy.

1-27 General Henry H. (Hap) Arnold, commander of the U.S. Army Air Forces, chats with Major General Louis E. Woods, USMC, commander of the Nineteenth Army Tactical Air Force on Okinawa during 1945. This organization had both Army and Marine aircraft. Arnold was responsible for B-29 modification, ballistic tests, and organization and training of the field unit selected to deliver the bomb.

H. H. (Hap) Arnold (1–27), commanding the Army Air Forces, had instructed that any Silver Plate request was to be filled immediately and without question.

General Ent had selected the 393rd Bomb Squadron as the nucleus of Tibbets's new outfit, the 509th Composite Group. Tibbets was happy to have this fully manned, equipped, and trained unit, and its squadron commander, Lieutenant Colonel Tom Classen, became his deputy. In addition to the Group Headquarters and the 393rd, which handled the tactical phase of the mission, the following units belonged to the 509th at its activation on December 17, 1944:

> 320th Troop Carrier Squadron, responsible for transporting troops and supplies between stateside stations and overseas
>
> Headquarters and Base Service Squadron, 390th Air Service Group, in charge of housing and administration. Under the 390th, the 603rd Air Engineer Squadron and 1027th Air Matériel Squadron provided "personnel and facilities to meet every conceivable problem" in their respective fields
>
> 1395th Military Police Company (Avn), responsible for security

On March 6, 1945, the 1st Ordnance Squadron, Special, Aviation, joined the team (1–28). It comprised hand-picked machinists, welders, and maintenance workers.

Tibbets had virtual carte blanche in personnel assignments, and gathered around him a group whose expertise and courage he trusted. Bombardier Major Thomas J. Ferebee (1–29) and navigator Captain Theodore J. (Dutch) Van Kirk had served with Tibbets in Europe. Other selectees included Major Charles W. (Chuck)

Sweeney (1–30), who replaced Classen in command of the 393rd. Captain Kermit K. Beahan was such a clever bombardier that he had been nicknamed "The Great Artiste." The enlisted crewmen were equally experienced and capable.

While these officers and men had met the required standards for service with B-29s, that was not good

1-28: 509th Composite Group Organization

509th Composite Group
  Col. Paul W. Tibbets, Jr., commanding officer
  Lt. Col. Thomas J. Classen, deputy commanding officer
  Lt. Col. Gerald E. Bean, executive officer
    390th Air Service Group
      Maj. John W. Porter
    393rd Bombardment Squadron (VH)
      Maj. Charles W. Sweeney
    1027th Air Matériel Squadron
      Maj. Guy Geller
    Headquarters and Base Service Squadron
      Maj. George W. Wescott
    1st Ordnance Squadron, Special (Aviation)
      Capt. Charles F. H. Begg
    320th Troop Carrier Squadron
      Capt. John W. Casey, Jr.
    603rd Air Engineering Squadron
      Capt. Earl O. Casey
    1395th M.P. Company (Aviation)
      Capt. Louis Schaffer
    1st Technical Detachment, War Department
      Miscellaneous Group

1-29 Major Thomas W. Ferebee, the group's lead bombardier under Colonel Tibbets.

1-30 Major Charles W. Sweeney, commanding officer, 393rd Bombardment Squadron.

enough for Tibbets. His demands for bombing from 30,000 feet with a circular error limit of 200 feet, and for no more than a half-mile margin of navigational error, seemed little short of insane. But Ferebee and Van Kirk proved it could be done. Accustomed to the conventional cylindrical bombs, the men were surprised to be confronted with a generally spherical shape. They would have to determine by experiment the best trajectory and

shape of the perfected bomb. In the interests of maneuverability and increased altitude, Tibbets insisted that the 509th's B-29s be stripped of turrets, guns, and all armor plate except the tail.

Some training took place far from Wendover. For a time, Tibbets tested newly delivered B-29s at Eglin Field, Florida (1–31). On January 7, 1945, an advance group that included six officers and twenty-six enlisted

1-31 Eglin Field, Florida, shown here on April 4, 1942.

1–32 The operations building and aircraft parking area at Batista Airport on December 26, 1943, located about ten miles south-southwest of Havana. Note the tile roof of the operations building in the foreground. In the parking area beyond lie a C-47 and two B-25s, likely G and C versions.

men of the 393rd left Wendover for Batista Field, Cuba (1–32). By the fourteenth, ten B-29s with their combat and group crews had arrived for specialized training, first in radar bombing and gunnery, and second for simulated combat missions. Training had been completed by the end of the month, leaving all concerned so in need of a rest that much of March and April was devoted to furloughs.

By April 26, 1945, the 509th was ready to proceed to the overseas location. The main group echelon traveled by train and troopship, reaching Tinian Island (1–33) on the afternoon of May 29. The Advanced Air Echelon traveled in three C-54s, the first of which began its movement on May 15. The second aircraft followed within the hour, but the third was delayed until May 19. All had reached Tinian by the twenty-second. From then on until the first week of August, men and equipment continued to arrive from the States.

Meanwhile, much had happened and continued to happen. The Battle of the Bulge gave the Allies a thought-provoking lesson in how much life could remain in an obviously defeated foe who refused to die without a fight. Dr. Bush had discussed the atom bomb with General Walter Bedell Smith, Eisenhower's Chief of Staff, who thought that the Germans' "desperate resistance" might possibly be "based upon the expectation of a successful development on their part of the weapon." But Bush did not agree, believing that the Germans had reached "the latter stages of the experimental process" but had not as yet "embarked on the highly expensive production."

Obviously, as the project advanced, more and more people perforce were admitted to the secret, and each one, however patriotic and trustworthy, represented one more possible leak. Moreover, Stimson was increasingly worried about the Soviet Union. On December 31, 1944, he told Roosevelt that the Russians were spying on the project but had not yet obtained any "real knowledge." Stimson had no illusions that the United States could keep such a secret permanently, but he did not want to take the Russians into the United States' confidence until the Americans could "get a real quid pro quo."

Up to this point, Stimson's invaluable diary gives no indication of any qualms on his part about the project. One has the impression that it was one more assignment, albeit a very important one, in a career of public service that extended back to the administration of President William Howard Taft. In his entry of March 3, 1945, however, he revealed how seriously he took his responsibility:

> We are up against some very big decisions. The time is approaching when we dare no longer avoid them and when events may force us into the public on the subject. Our thoughts went right back to the bottom facts on human nature, morals and government, and it is by far the most searching and important thing that I have had to do since I have been here in the office of the Secretary of War because it touches matters which are deeper even than the principles of present government.

On April 12, 1945, Roosevelt died and Harry S. Truman became president. Stimson and Groves briefed him on

1–33 B-29s parked on the hardstand at North Field on the island of Tinian in 1945. The field was developed on the location of the former Japanese Ushi Point airfield. The Americans used the beaches in the foreground in the invasion of the island.

April 25 concerning the Manhattan Project, of which Truman had known nothing. The new president remembered his passage-at-arms with Stimson and acknowledged that the latter could have taken no other course.

On May 7 came the long-awaited surrender of Germany. Two days later, Truman's Interim Committee on Nuclear Energy held its first meeting. Stimson chaired the eight-member group, which included such project veterans as Conant, Karl Compton, and Vannevar Bush. Others were Under Secretary of the Navy Ralph A. Bard (1–34); Assistant Secretary of State for Economic Affairs William L. Clayton; George L. Harrison, the president of the New York Life Insurance Company, Stimson's special assistant in regard to the atomic bomb

1–34 Ralph A. Bard (right) chats with Fleet Admiral Chester W. Nimitz during the U.S. Naval Academy's centennial ceremonies in the second week of October 1945.

1–35 James F. Byrnes (third from left) attends a meeting in 1945 with (l–r) Navy Joint Chief Fleet Admiral William D. Leahy, former Chief of Naval Operations Admiral Harold R. Stark, Ambassador to Belgium Sawyer, President Harry S. Truman, General Dwight D. Eisenhower, and naval aide to the president Captain James K. Vardaman, Jr.

project; and James F. Byrnes (1–35), who represented Truman on the committee.

The Interim Committee met for an important two-day session on May 31 and June 1. In addition to the membership, four physicist advisers were present—Oppenheimer, Fermi, Arthur H. Compton, and Ernest O. Lawrence (see photo 1–7) of the Radiation Laboratory at the University of California at Berkeley. Also in attendance was the Army chief of staff, General George C. Marshall (1–36). Of all Truman's and Stimson's subordinates, none enjoyed more of their trust and respect than Marshall, so it was not surprising that Stimson wanted him present.

What was surprising was Marshall's suggestion that some scientists from the Soviet Union might be invited to observe the anticipated atomic bomb test. This proposal met with unanimous rejection. The committee reached three conclusions: The bomb should be used as soon as possible, without warning, against a Japanese city where war plants were set amidst workers' homes and other easily damaged buildings, in order to create the greatest possible psychological impact. Earlier, Marshall had thought that the bomb should be used against either a purely military objective or a manufacturing center, with the population warned in advance. But on this occasion he had either changed his mind or did not feel he was in a position to object, not being a member of the committee.

A good case could be made for withholding a warning. There were fears that with such advance notice the Japanese would move masses of prisoners of war into the threatened area. And there were such things as dud bombs. If the proclaimed superweapon fizzled out, the United States would look exceedingly foolish.

Despite Germany's surrender, Japan still fought on with grim determination. During a firebombing of Tokyo on the night of March 9–10, over 100,000 had perished—more than would die in either atomic blast—yet

1-36 General George C. Marshall (left center) chats with Lord Halifax, Admiral Ernest J. King, and Bernard M. Baruch during the Navy Day Dinner at the Waldorf-Astoria Hotel, New York City, on October 27, 1944.

the Japanese war effort did not break stride. The Americans were winning in the Pacific, but at a horrific cost. The struggle for Okinawa continued to rage.

Yet in the small circle of those in the know, doubts as to the wisdom and practicality of the project arose. Szilard feared that using the bomb would trigger an ultimately disastrous arms race with the Soviet Union. Oppenheimer suggested to Byrnes that deaths from the bomb would be around 20,000—far fewer than could be expected from a conventional air raid. To Szilard Oppenheimer declared, to the former's astonishment, that the atomic bomb had "no military significance." Admiral William D. Leahy (1–37), who had been Roosevelt's personal chief of staff, told Truman that "the damn thing" would never work. It was all "bunk."

1-37 Fleet Admiral William D. Leahy, a great skeptic concerning the atom bomb project.

CHAPTER 2

Plans and Preparations

Untroubled by theoretical or political considerations, the 509th settled down on Tinian as part of the 313th Bombardment Wing, XXI Bomber Command. These commands, however, had only administrative authority over the 509th, because Groves was not about to lose his control over the atomic bomb. He sent his deputy, Brigadier Geneneral Thomas F. Farrell (2–1), to Tinian along with two Los Alamos scientists. These the 509th called the "Tinian Joint Chiefs." Through them would come the "go" or "no go" signal direct from Truman to Groves to Farrell. Heavy drapes isolated the teletype machine over which this message would come.

2-1 The Manhattan Project's deputy director, Brigadier General Thomas F. Farrell, in his office on Tinian in 1945.

Tinian Island was a scrap of land about twelve miles long by six and a half miles wide. North Field, where the 509th was stationed, had four runways. For some time, life there was a sort of glorified camping out (2–2). The men washed their own clothes and cut each other's hair. Their helmets held their shaving water. At first they were not permitted to leave the compound, but this restriction was lifted shortly.

Soon more civilized conditions prevailed. In July, the group moved into a former Seabee area where they acquired such amenities as eighty-nine Quonset huts (2–3), a mess hall, and "sufficient latrine, shower, and water facilities." They now had a chapel and an outdoor theater named "Pumpkin Playhouse" in obvious tribute to the group's pumpkin-shaped bombs. The Twentieth Air Force cooperated to expedite construction, including storage and laboratory facilities for the bomb (2–4).

Meanwhile, in June, the 509th's last unit joined. This was the 1st Technical Service Detachment, War Department Miscellaneous Group. Its assignment was to administer "a variety of scientists, security officers and Naval personnel" needed for the project. These included physicians to determine the physiological effects of the mission on both crew members and the Japanese, Navy officers "who aided in designing the bomb," counterintelligence personnel, fuse experts, radar operators and some of "the vast numbers of scientists" who had done so much to bring the project to fruition.

Training at Tinian began promptly. Upon arrival, all combat personnel attended the Wing Lead Crew Ground School for seven days. There they were indoctrinated in a wide variety of subjects listed in the unit history as "Theater History, Air Sea Rescue, Ditching and Bailouts Survival, Japanese people, Radar Bombing

2-2 Tent quarters at North Field, March 28, 1945.

2-3 Quonset huts near North Field on Tinian. Similar buildings found use as offices and briefing rooms.

2-4 Colonel Elmer E. Kilpatrick, Twentieth Air Force engineer, who expedited construction at Tinian.

2-5 Iwo Jima, May 26, 1945, looking toward Mount Suribachi. Note the B-29s parked on the airfield.

Methods, Wing and AAF regulations, Weather, Cruise Control, Emergency Procedures, Camera Operation, Dinghy Drill," and other classes bearing directly on combat operations.

The 313th Wing's required training missions included a four-and-a-half-hour instrument calibration and orientation flight; an eight-hour navigational mission to Iwo Jima (2–5), bombing Rota (2–6) on the way back; a two-hour local night mission; two four-hour flights over Rota for radar and visual bombing; and "a shakedown bombing mission on Truk" (2–7).

Five training missions were flown before the first combat flight. The following chart (2–8) lists the 509th's aircraft commanders. The first of these missions, on July 6, targeted the two runways on Marcus Island. The aircraft crews were headed by Captains Ralph R. Taylor, Jr., and George W. Marquand, and Lieutenant Ralph N. Devore, with results judged good to excellent. The next day, the aircraft captained by Captains Taylor, John A. Wilson, and Frederick C. Bock, Jr., and Lieutenants Joseph E. Westover and Devore flew a similar mission with similar results. Another group, with pilots Captains

2-6 Aircraft from USS *White Plains* (CVE-66) sink a Japanese transport off Rota in the Marianas on June 24, 1944.

2-7 Aerial reconnaissance photo of Truk taken by a PB4Y-1 patrol bomber on February 4, 1944. Eten Island airfield lies at center, with a multitude of warships and merchantmen anchored in the vicinity.

Claude R. (Buck) Eatherly, James N. Price, Marquand, and Bock, and Lieutenant Charles F. McKnight, put on a repeat performance. This time four aircraft bombed by radar "with unobserved results"; the fifth, bombing visually, had excellent results. A series of practice bombing runs over Rota and Guam followed.

Of course, the 509th's seventeen B-29s, with their distinctive insignia of an encircled black arrow, going their mysterious ways, aroused "curiosity concerning the missions of the 509th . . . within the other outfits stationed

2-8: Aircraft Commanders, 509th Composite Group

Col. Paul W. Tibbets, Jr. group commander	Capt. Ralph N. Devore
Lt. Col. Thomas J. Classen deputy group commander	Capt. Robert A. Lewis
Maj. Charles W. Sweeney squadron commander	Capt. George W. Marquand
Maj. Claude R. Eatherly	Capt. Charles F. McKnight
Maj. Ralph R. Taylor, Jr.	Capt. James N. Price, Jr.
Maj. John A. Wilson	Capt. Norman W. Ray
Capt. Frederick C. Bock, Jr.	Capt. Joseph E. Westover
Capt. Edward M. Costello	Capt. Herman S. Zahn, Jr.

on the island," observes the unit history sedately, "in the form of whispered speculation." Any group or individual operating outside the rules of its milieu is likely to arouse, at worst, suspicious resentment and, at best, a sort of good-natured sarcasm. This bit of verse authored by a clerk in Base Operations is typical:

> Into the air the secret rose,
> Where they're going, nobody knows.
> Tomorrow they'll return again
> But we'll never know where they've been.
> Don't ask us about results or such
> Unless you want to get in Dutch.
> But take it from the one who is sure of the score,
> The 509th is winning the war.

The formation and training of the 509th were predicated upon the premise that the atomic bomb could be effective and would be used. This was still an iffy proposition, but the U.S. Army Air Forces could not wait for a successful test and a firm "go" signal before beginning preparations. A force in being had to be in place and prepared when and if the word came. Hence the 509th.

But other options had to be considered. Some influential and knowledgeable individuals, such as Major General Curtis E. LeMay (2–9), at the time deputy commander of the Twentieth Air Force, and former ambassador to Japan Joseph C. Grew (2–10), believed that a continuation of the massive strategic bombing effort against Japan's cities was the best method of forcing that

2-9 Major General Curtis E. LeMay, deputy commander, Twentieth Air Force. He took over as General Spaatz's chief of staff on August 1, 1945.

2-10 Former ambassador to Japan Joseph C. Grew conducts a press conference at Pearl Harbor on November 16, 1944.

nation's surrender. Certainly it was difficult to imagine that the Japanese could stand up indefinitely against punishment such as Tokyo had experienced, documented by postwar photos 2–11, 2–12, and 2–13, taken respectively on August 25 and 27, and September 9, 1945.

Admiral Leahy favored a bombing offensive combined with naval blockade. And, of course, it might come to a direct invasion of Japan, an alternative that those involved in top planning viewed with no enthusiasm. In view of the courage the Japanese had demonstrated in defending the stepping-stone island approaches, no one doubted that their defense of the actual home soil would be even more desperate, even fanatical. Total U.S. casualties from an invasion were unpredictable, but could run as high as one million. Estimates for the first thirty days ranged from about 31,000 to 50,000.

Still, unpalatable as the prospect might be, this option had to be considered. The strategy that Marshall presented to the Joint Chiefs, which they adopted on June 18, received the overall code name of Downfall. It postulated air bombardment and naval blockade of Japan from bases on Okinawa, Iwo Jima, the Marianas, and the Philippines to soften the Home Islands for invasion, instead of being the direct instrument of victory. Then, on November 1, 1945, would begin Operation Olympic, the assault on Kyushu, with accompanying intensification of the bombing and blockade. The final invasion of the heart of Japan, code-named Coronet, would begin on March 1, 1946, with an assault on the main Home Island, Honshu, centering on the Kanto Plain around Tokyo.

Oddly enough, no mention was made of the atomic bomb until the meeting was breaking up. Truman stopped Assistant Secretary of War John J. McCloy and

2-11 Firebomb damage to a residential and commercial section of Tokyo.

2-12 Destruction in downtown Tokyo of the older wood structures is total; only concrete masonry buildings survive.

2-13 Further devastation in Tokyo as a result of incendiary bombing raids.

asked for his opinion. McCloy turned to Stimson, who told him to go ahead. McCloy suggested that the invasion might be avoided. The United States could tell Japan about the bomb, stressing just what kind of weapon it was, then present surrender terms. Those terms would include retention of the Emperor. Even if Japan refused, the American "moral position" would be strengthened by the warning.

On July 4, a milestone toward use of the bomb was passed when Stimson, Groves, Bush, and other Americans met with a group of British dignitaries and secured the agreement of both nations to use the bomb against Japan. Three days later, Truman boarded the cruiser *Augusta* bound for the Potsdam Conference (2–14). Stimson had preceded him by air. Thus the two top officials

2-14 President Truman debarks from USS *Augusta* (CA-31) at Antwerp, Belgium, en route to the Potsdam Conference, July 15, 1945, followed by Secretary of State James F. Byrnes.

2-15 Control house and observation post at Alamogordo. The test bomb, transported via the roadway at right, would be detonated from this point. Note the shadow of the aircraft carrying the Signal Corps photographer who took this picture.

concerned were out of the country when the long-awaited moment came to test the atom bomb. Photo 2–15 shows the control house and observation post at Alamogordo where the bomb would be detonated.

The world's first nuclear explosion occurred at 5:29 A.M., Monday, July 16, 1945. It promptly erased any doubts that "the damn thing" would work (2–16). The bomb evaporated the steel tower atop which it was exploded, and destroyed a test construction of steel set in concrete that no one had expected to be damaged because it was half a mile away. The light was visible up to some 180 miles away, the sound heard at about a hundred miles' distance. The ball of fire rose over 10,000 feet, and the cloud generated soared about 36,000 feet above ground level. It was truly an awesome sight that left no observer unmoved. Into Oppenheimer's mind flashed words from the *Bhagavad-Gita*: "Now I am become Death, the destroyer of worlds" (2–17). Nevertheless, all concerned were enormously relieved that their years of work and expenditure of roughly $2 billion had paid off in a weapon that conceivably could win the war.

Stimson received a message on the sixteenth, "very general" in nature, of the successful test. Details came in on the eighteenth; Stimson took them to Truman, "who was highly delighted." Less pleased was Eisenhower, whose immediate reaction was the hope that the United States would not be the first to introduce into war anything as "horrible and destructive as this weapon was described to be." Later, however, he admitted that this was a personal reaction without analysis of the situation.

One who had no such qualms when Stimson gave him the details was Winston Churchill. To him the bomb represented deliverance from a nightmare—assault upon and invasion of the Japanese homeland, which might well cost "a million American lives and half that number of British," not to mention enemy losses. Perhaps the Japanese might find in "this almost supernatural weapon" a way to surrender with honor.

The 509th's training on Tinian had moved into an operational phase. Fourteen plans had been prepared, each prescribing "a pin-point target." These were usually strategic industries in or near a medium-sized town. Target-study classes were set up so that the crews concerned could become familiar with their assigned targets and receive any other information that might be helpful in accomplishing their mission.

A flurry of activity enlivened July 19. Target classes were held; crews were encouraged to ask "last-minute questions"; the staff held special briefings. At a general briefing, Tibbets wished the selected crews good luck, and "reminded them that the eyes of the 313th Wing were upon them." At two A.M., July 21, the first B-29s took to the air, this time to drop their "pumpkin-colored, pumpkin-shaped bombs" on targets in the Japanese Home Islands.

This initial mission was by no means a rousing success. Of the ten aircraft participating, one experienced engine failure and had to jettison its bomb at sea. Five crews struck their primary targets, two by radar, three visually. Four had to settle for radar strikes on targets of

2-16 Five-thirty A.M., July 16, 1945. Success—explosion of the test device at Alamogordo. Unless there should be some last-minute capitulation by the Japanese, the mushroom cloud rendered moot further discussions of war options.

2-17 Crater and scorch marks left behind by the world's first nuclear detonation. Note the road at left, which terminates at ground zero.

opportunity. One of these was Eatherly's aircraft, *Straight Flush*. In a most ill-advised move, this crew selected Tokyo as their target, dropping their bomb either on the palace grounds or upon a nearby railroad station (the later accounts of the crewmen do not agree on this point). Nor is it clear whether this particular crew had instructions to avoid the palace area. There is no question, however, that avoidance was the overall policy and well understood.

The possibilities inherent in this foolish action are staggering. If Eatherly's bomb had happened to kill the Emperor (2–18), the forces within Japan that were working cautiously toward surrender would have lost their best, most influential ally, and the militarists would have had a made-to-order rallying point for a last-ditch resistance.

2-18 H.I.M. Hirohito, Emperor of Japan.

All aircraft returned to Tinian safely, with results rated "Fair to Unobserved." As the unit history remarked, "Quiet disappointment and an aggrieved anxiety could be sensed in all concerned." One fact was abundantly clear: All their technical expertise, meticulous training, and thorough indoctrination meant little or nothing unless the weather cooperated. On this day's run, visibility had been miserable, and results showed it.

The weather on July 23 was fine, and the ten aircraft of the second mission performed well, with results rated "Effective and Successful." Tibbets received a warm message of congratulations from the commanding general of the 313th Bombardment Wing, Brigadier General John H. Davies (see photo 3–2).

During the last days of July, the 509th hit the Japanese homeland two more times. Heavy cloud cover plagued the first of these missions, and none of the ten aircraft could bomb its primary target. Results on secondary targets were evaluated a "successful, but fair as to effectiveness."

The last mission, held on July 29, saw the only major accident of the 509th's overseas tour of duty. The "pumpkin" broke loose from one B-29, thudding into the hardstand. Fortunately, no one was working under the plane at the time, but the aircraft had to be left behind. The weather smiled again, and the eight remaining crews could bomb visually, four their primary and four their secondary targets.

According to the unit historian, the first week of August "was filled with much off-the-record scurrying about, secret meetings, and conferences behind closed doors." In photo 2–19, combat crew members listen intently during a target-study class of August 1. Photo 2-20 shows that while the men were attentive, the atmosphere was relaxed and informal. Captain Joseph D. Buscher lectures in photo 2–21, apparently undisturbed

2-19 Combat crews of the 393rd Bombardment Squadron during a target-study class on August 1, 1945. In the front-row seats are (l-r) Captain Norman W. Ray; Second Lieutenant John E. Cantlon; Captain Frederick C. Bock, Jr.; and Second Lieutenant Paul W. Gruning.

2-20 The men have shifted their seating somewhat. Identified officers are (l-r) Major Ralph R. Taylor, Jr.; Lieutenant Cantlon; Major John A. Wilson; Lieutenant Gruning; First Lieutenant Michael Angelich (behind Gruning's knee), Second Lieutenant Jacob Y. Bontekoe, and First Lieutenant Williamson (scribbling in his notepad).

2-21 Captain Joseph D. Buscher, from group headquarters, continues his lecture while the photographer moves to the back of the Quonset hut. Lieutenant Gruning is relaxed, his leg slung onto the table at right.

2-22 Lieutenant Charles Levy takes over to discuss a different target.

by the movements of the camera. Soon Lieutenant Charles Levy, a member of Bock's crew, took the floor to discuss a different target (2–22). The whole atmosphere is that of men who know their business and are confident they can carry it out.

A comparable surge of activity had been taking place at decision-making level. The list of target cities must be firmed up. One criterion was that these cities should have so far been relatively untouched. This was to ensure that the results of the atom bomb could not be charged up to previous conventional bombings. This condition

alone ruled out a good half-dozen major cities. And of course the target had to contain, as the Joint Committee had specified, "a military installation or war plant."

Hap Arnold originally nominated Kyoto, Hiroshima, Kokura, and Niigata. With Truman's hearty concurrence, Stimson promptly removed Kyoto from the list, for this was Japan's old capitol, a city with many historic, cultural, and religious sites.

On July 24, Truman, still at the Potsdam Conference, ordered the bomb delivered as soon as the weather permitted after August 3. The War Department forwarded the decision with instructions to General Carl A. (Tooey) Spaatz, who had become commander of the U.S. Strategic Air Forces on July 16 (2–23). Spaatz would be responsible for delivery of the bomb (2–24). Lieutenant General Nathan F. Twining (2–25), who assumed command of the Twentieth Air Force on August 1, would issue field orders for the atomic missions.

The project still could have been canceled had Japan given any signs of accepting the Potsdam Proclamation (2–26). This historic proclamation, which reached Tokyo on July 26, called for Japan's unconditional surrender with terms roughly as follows:

1. Permanent elimination of the power and influence of the military.
2. Allied forces would occupy key places until a "new order of peace, security and justice" had been established.
3. Japanese sovereignty would be limited to the Home Islands. In other words, Japan must give up all territory taken by aggression since she had been forced out of isolation in 1853.
4. Japan's military forces would be disarmed, then permitted to return to their homes with the opportunity "to lead to peaceful and productive lives."
5. Justice would be meted out to war criminals but there was no intention to enslave Japan. "Freedom of

2-23 General Carl A. (Tooey) Spaatz, the field commander responsible for delivery of the atomic bomb.

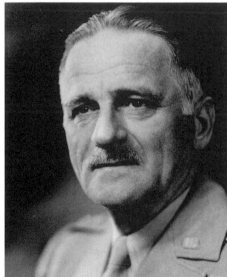

2-25 Lieutenant General Nathan F. Twining, commanding general, Twentieth Air Force.

2-24 Letter from General Thomas T. Handy to Spaatz, authorizing use of the atomic bombs then on Tinian.

WAR DEPARTMENT
OFFICE OF THE CHIEF OF STAFF
WASHINGTON 25, D.C

25 July 1945

TO: General Carl Spaatz
       Commanding General
       United States Army Strategic Air Forces

1. The 509 Composite Group, 20th Air Force will deliver its first special bomb as soon as weather will permit visual bombing after about 3 August 1945 on one of the targets: Hiroshima, Kokura, Niigata and Nagasaki. To carry military and civilian scientific personnel from the War Department to observe and record the effects of the explosion of the bomb, additional aircraft will accompany the airplane carrying the bomb. The observing planes will stay several miles distant from the point of impact of the bomb.

2. Additional bombs will be delivered on the above targets as soon as made ready by the project staff. Further instructions will be issued concerning targets other than those listed above.

3. Dissemination of any and all information concerning the use of the weapon against Japan is reserved to the Secretary of War and the President of the United States. No communiques on the subject or releases of information will be issued by Commanders in the field without specific prior authority. Any news stories will be sent to the War Department for special clearance.

4. The foregoing directive is issued to you by direction and with the approval of the Secretary of War and of the Chief of Staff, USA. It is desired that you personally deliver one copy of this directive to General MacArthur and one copy to Admiral Nimitz for their information.

THOS. T. HANDY
General, G.S.C.
Acting Chief of Staff

2-26 The "Big Three" at Potsdam (l-r): Prime Minister Clement Attlee; President Harry S. Truman; and Premier Joseph Stalin. China signed the Potsdam Declaration; the U.S.S.R. did not.

speech, of religion, and of thought, as well as respect for the fundamental human rights" would be established.

6. Japan could retain an industrial base for her economy, but not rearm.
7. Occupation would end when Japan had "established a peacefully inclined and responsible government."
8. Japan must "proclaim now the unconditional surrender of all Japanese armed forces," on pain of "prompt and utter destruction."

The document made no mention of retention of the Emperor, despite the urging of Stimson, Grew, and others of like mind. There was too much anti-Emperor sentiment among the Allies to overcome.

2-27 Shigenori Togo, Japan's foreign minister.

The Japanese Foreign Ministry gave this document a careful, almost word-by-word analysis. Two points seemed hopeful. First, the Soviet Union had not signed, so maintained neutrality. Thus Japan's current efforts to secure Moscow as a peace intermediary could continue. Second, the Cairo Declaration had called for the unconditional surrender of Japan, whereas the Potsdam Declaration demanded the unconditional surrender of the Japanese armed forces—a very different thing.

Foreign Minister Shigenori Togo (2–27) thought the terms acceptable, but wanted to hold up an answer pending Moscow's reply to Japan's approaches. But General Korechika Anami (2–28), the minister of war, and General Yoshijiro Umezu, the army's chief of staff (2–29), wanted immediate rejection. As a compromise, the proclamation was published without official comment, but not before the military had insisted upon deletion of

2-28 General Korechika Anami, minister of war.

2-29 General Yoshijiro Umezu, army chief of staff.

2-30 Admiral Baron Kantaro Suzuki, prime minister of Japan.

any humane terminology. Then, on July 28, Prime Minister Admiral Baron Kantaro Suzuki (2–30) publicly announced that Japan would ignore the Potsdam Proclamation and continue to fight. This was a sad blunder and cost Japan dearly.

2-31 With mind made up, if not completely at ease, in the wake of Japan's rejection of the Potsdam Declaration, President Truman works in his wardroom on board *Augusta* during the return trip to the United States.

On August 2, the same day he left Potsdam for home (2–31), Truman gave the final green light to proceed with the atom bomb mission. By that time all the necessary parts for assembling the bomb were in place on Tinian. Weather was unfavorable the first few days of August; as of August 5, the 509th still had not received the strike order. Tibbets and his men, however, were loading and following their schedule, to be ready when the work did arrive. In the early evening, it came, from Groves to Farrell, as planned.

While these final preparations were taking place, a drama was played out at sea, an indirect part of the atomic bomb story. The cruiser *Indianapolis* (2–32) had been undergoing repairs at Mare Island Navy Yard when the tests at Alamogordo were completed. Promptly charged with the urgent mission of delivering to Tinian the fissionable material for the atomic bombs, she immediately departed San Francisco with her secret cargo.

She had an uneventful voyage to Tinian, where she delivered the atomic bomb components on July 26, 1945, no doubt glad to leave them in the care of the 1st Ordnance Squadron, Special (Aviation) (2–33). The cruiser left Tinian immediately (2–34), ordered to Guam, thence to Leyte, where she and her crew were to undergo training with Task Force 95 off Okinawa. *Indianapolis* reached Guam safely and on July 28 proceeded unescorted on a direct route to Leyte (2–35). Her skipper, Captain Charles S. McVay III, received instructions to zigzag "at discretion," which he did during the day, but not at night.

As the top-heavy old cruiser had no air-conditioning, McVay ordered ventilation trunks and bulkheads opened, as well as hatches to living spaces on the lower decks. The main and second decks were wide open. In

2–32 USS *Indianapolis* (CA-35) off Mare Island Navy Yard on July 10, 1945.

2–33 Captain Charles F. H. Begg, whose 1st Ordnance Squadron, Special (Aviation) acted as custodian of the bombs and their components on Tinian.

2–34 Last known photograph of *Indianapolis*. Taken as she prepared to depart Tinian after delivering atomic bomb components.

2-35 Track of *Indianapolis* on the voyage to Leyte that ended in her sinking.

that condition, she was about to encounter one of the Japanese navy's veteran submariners, Lieutenant Commander Mochitsura Hashimoto (2–36), skipper of the *kaiten* submarine *I-58* (2–37), which was equipped with midget craft similar to those used at Pearl Harbor.

Routine patrols had proved fruitless until Hashimoto opted to place his boat where the routes from Guam and Leyte and Peleliu to Okinawa intersected. At this crossroads American ships were certain to pass. Sure enough, he sighted *Indianapolis* silhouetted five miles distant at about 11:05 P.M. Tokyo time. Hashimoto submerged and

2-36 Former lieutenant commander Mochitsura Hashimoto, commander of *kaiten* submarine *I-58*, examines a navigation chart at the court-martial of Captain McVay.

2-37 Japanese submarine *I-58* at Sasebo after the war, January 28, 1946.

2–38 Forward torpedo room of *I-58.*

prepared to fire. By 11:32 *Indianapolis* was only 1,500 yards distant. Hashimoto did not even have to use his midgets; he loosed a spread of six torpedoes (2–38).

Two of these struck *Indianapolis* abreast the Number 1 turret and under the wardroom. The violent explosions that followed ripped open the cruiser's bottom and severed communications and fire mains. McVay ordered distress signals sent, but there is no evidence that any station picked them up. As the ship's list increased, McVay ordered the crew to abandon ship. *Indianapolis* slipped bow first beneath the choppy sea at approximately 12:12 A.M. on July 30 (local time), carrying about 400 of her crew with her. In the confusion of abandoning ship, only six life rafts and as many float nets found their way into the water. During the long first night, fifty to

one hundred of the most badly wounded men perished.

For four days the men languished in the shark-infested waters, many with severe burns and all suffering from exposure, thirst, and despair. Passing aircraft repeatedly ignored the men, even though the sailors frequently fired flares. Finally, at ten A.M. on Thursday, August 2, while flying a routine search out of Peleliu, Lieutenant (j.g.) Wilbur C. Swinn, the pilot of a land-based PV-1 Ventura, sighted *Indianapolis*'s stranded survivors. Soon two PBY patrol bombers appeared and landed in the water nearby, taking on fifty-seven men. Rescue ships arrived beginning at midnight of August 2–3, and stayed in the vicinity for five days searching for survivors. The last group (which included McVay) came on board *Ringness* (APD-100) (2–39) around noon on August 3.

2–39 USS *Ringness* (APD-100).

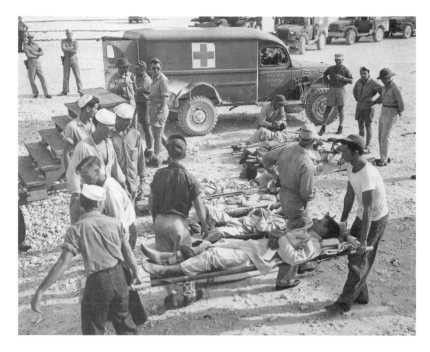

2-40 *Indianapolis* survivors en route to a hospital (probably on Guam) in early August 1945. The ambulance in the background is marked "U.S.N. Base Hospital Nº 20."

Excluding those who were rescued but later died from injuries and exposure, only 316 men from *Indianapolis* survived their ordeal, leaving 883 dead. At least 484 died in the water (2–40 and 2–41). These men may well be considered casualties of the atomic bomb operation—as it turned out, the only American casualties.

2-41 Following his voyage to Guam on board high-speed transport *Ringess,* Captain McVay recounts the sinking of *Indianapolis* to war correspondents in August 1945.

CHAPTER 3

Target Number One

Training was over; "pumpkin" strikes were over; the mission was at hand. Captain William S. Parsons, USN, the weaponeer, briefed the crews on August 4. He had planned to show movies of the Alamogordo test, but the briefing room was too small for the film to focus, so he settled for still photographs. The word "atomic" was not mentioned, but the stills lent force to Parsons's description of the bomb as the most powerful ever created. At this briefing, Tibbets stressed that the top brass believed that this single bomb "might shorten the war by six months." It is not clear whether Parsons spoke of radioactivity, but he did warn the crews to stay away from the cloud the blast would generate.

Two briefings were held on August 5, the final one just before midnight, behind locked doors guarded by MPs. Tibbets, Parsons, and Classen (3–1) gave detailed instructions. There was still no mention of the bomb's nature, but at least one of those present stated that the men knew it anyway. Group chaplain William F. Downey offered a brief prayer that the

3-1 Manhattan Project and mission leaders meet on Tinian in August 1945 (l–r): Rear Admiral William R. Purnell, technical adviser; Brigadier General Thomas F. Farrell, deputy director of the Manhattan Project; Colonel Paul W. Tibbets, Jr., commanding officer, 509th Composite Group; Captain William S. Parsons, USN, weaponeer on the Hiroshima mission.

3-2 Crew of group commander Tibbets. Standing (l-r): Second Lieutenant Morris Jeppson; Captain Robert A. Lewis; Brigadier General John H. Davies (commanding general, 313th Bombardment Wing); Colonel Tibbets; Major Thomas W. Ferebee; Captain Parsons. Kneeling (l-r): Staff Sergeant Wyatt E. Duzenbury; Sergeant Joseph A. Stiborik; Captain Theodore J. Van Kirk; Staff Sergeant George R. Caron; Sergeant Robert R. Shumard; Private First Class Richard H. Nelson. Not pictured is First Lieutenant Jacob Beser, radar countermeasures officer.

war might end soon and the men return safely from their mission.

Pre-takeoff and actual takeoff events were in almost comical contrast to the super hush-hush atmosphere that had surrounded the project. Up until August 1, public relations had been assigned to First Lieutenant Frederick C. Krug, weather officer of the 393rd, as an additional duty. The task could not have been onerous, with the whole group operating under a news blackout. Captain Joseph D. Buscher replaced Krug on August 1, and by midnight of August 5 had more than enough to do.

Dozens of cameramen surged around to take pictures of the crews. Naturally Tibbets and his men were prime targets (3–2).

Seven B-29s would participate in the initial mission. One was spotted at Iwo Jima as a spare, in case another plane experienced trouble en route. Three were to determine over which of three targets the weather was most clear. *Full House,* piloted by Captain Ralph R. Taylor, Jr., covered Kokura, and *Jabbit III,* captained by Major John A. Wilson, scouted Nagasaki. The weather plane for Hiroshima, the principal target, was Eatherly's

Straight Flush. These three would advise the strike aircraft of their findings. The fourth target city, Niigata, had been omitted from this mission as not big enough to warrant the longer flight north.

Tibbets piloted the strike aircraft, which he had named *Enola Gay* in honor of his mother. Two escort aircraft, one under Sweeney, the other piloted by Marquand, accompanied *Enola Gay,* each with camera equipment, and one "carried special instruments of a highly scientific nature," in the unit history's words (3–3). Tibbets considered the mission of the escorts fully as important as his own, for they were under orders to collect scientific data. After the drop, the escorts would release parachutes bearing the instruments. Moreover, each carried scientific observers to measure and evaluate the blast.

Cameras continued to click as if reluctant to miss a single shot. Among those watching Tibbets's crew board *Enola Gay* was the prestigious *New York Times* correspondent William L. Laurence, no doubt wishing that he could join them on one of the greatest news stories of the century (3–4). Nor could the fliers' fellow officers resist the opportunity to hobnob with a group of men almost

3-3: Crew Members for Hiroshima Mission—August 6, 1945

Enola Gay, Victor 82

Col. Paul W. Tibbets, Jr.	Group Commander and Pilot
Capt. Robert A. Lewis	Copilot
Capt. William S. Parsons, USN	Weaponeer
Capt. Theodore J. Van Kirk	Navigator
Maj. Thomas W. Ferebee	Bombardier
1st Lt. Jacob Beser	Radar Countermeasures
2nd Lt. Morris Jeppson*	Electronics Officer/Assistant Weaponeer
S/Sgt. Wyatt E. Duzenbury	Flight Engineer
S/Sgt. George R. Caron	Tail Gunner
Sgt. Joseph A. Stiborik	Radio Operator
Sgt. Robert R. Shumard	Aviation Mechanic/Gunner/Assistant Flight Engineer
Pfc. Richard H. Nelson	Radio Operator

The Great Artiste, Victor 89

Maj. Charles W. Sweeney	Squadron Commander and Pilot
1st Lt. Charles D. Albury	Copilot
Capt. James F. Van Pelt, Jr.	Navigator
Capt. Kermit K. Beahan	Bombardier
M/Sgt. John D. Kuharek	Flight Engineer
S/Sgt. Edward R. Buckley	Radar Operator
Sgt. Abe M. Spitzer	Radio Operator
Sgt. Albert T. DeHart	Tail Gunner
Sgt. Raymond G. Gallagher	Aviation Mechanic/Gunner
Dr. Luis W. Alvarez†	Scientific Observer
Lawrence H. Johnston†	Scientific Observer
Harold Agnew†	Scientific Observer

Unnamed Escort Aircraft, Victor 91

Capt. George W. Marquand	Pilot
Capt. James W. Strudwick	Bombardier
2nd Lt. James W. Anderson	Copilot
2nd Lt. Russell Gackenbach	Navigator
T/Sgt. James R. Corliss	Flight Engineer
Sgt. Warren L. Coble	Radio Operator
Cpl. Joseph M. DiJulio	Radar Operator
Cpl. Melvin H. Bierman	Tail Gunner
Cpl. Anthony D. Capua Gunner	Aircraft Mechanic/
Prof. Bernard Waldman†	Scientific Observer

*Lt. Jeppson was borrowed from the 1st Ordnance Squadron.
†All four scientific observers were members of the 1st Technical Services Detachment at Tinian.

3-4 *New York Times* **correspondent William L. Laurence stands by the group public relations officer. Laurence would ride in** *The Great Artiste* **on the mission to Nagasaki. He would become a Pulitzer Prize winner.**

3-5 An unidentified officer chats with Ferebee, Tibbets, and Van Kirk. All seem in good spirits except for Bombardier Ferebee, who appears rather somber— perhaps because of the pressure and responsibility of personally delivering the bomb.

3-6 Bathed in the glare of klieg lights, Colonel Tibbets's crew poses with Major John W. Porter (ground operations officer and commanding officer of the 390th Air Service Group) before boarding *Enola Gay* early in the morning of August 6. Those present are, standing (l-r): Major Porter, Captain Van Kirk, Major Ferebee, Colonel Tibbets, Captain Lewis, and First Lieutenant Jacob Beser, in charge of radar countermeasures. Kneeling (l-r): Sergeant Stiborik, Staff Sergeant Caron, Private First Class Nelson, Sergeant Shumard, Staff Sergeant Duzenbury.

certain to make history (3–5). There had to be a last-minute photo of Tibbets's crew (3–6), although Parsons and his assistant, Second Lieutenant Morris Jeppson, were elsewhere, probably checking out the bomb in *Enola Gay* (3–7).

Nicknamed Little Boy, the bomb loaded into *Enola Gay* (3–8) was ten feet long, with a diameter of twenty-eight inches, and weighed about four tons. Two quantities of U-235 were placed inside, one in the nose, the other near the tail. Individually these quantities were not sufficient to cause fission, but when the gunpowder packed in the tail ignited, it would force the parts together and cause the explosion.

3-7 Perhaps pausing in his bomb-bay activities with Captain Parsons, Lieutenant Jeppson smiles for the cameraman and posterity before boarding.

3-8 The Hiroshima bomb, Little Boy, being placed in the bomb bay of *Enola Gay* at North Field on Tinian, August 5, 1945. Present (l-r) are Rear Admiral Purnell, Brigadier General Farrell, and Captain Parsons. At center, with hands on hips, is Dr. Norman Ramsey of the Los Alamos Technical Group.

3-9 Corporal Robert Behr assists with the takeoff broadcast.

The takeoff would be broadcast. One of those assisting was Corporal Robert Behr (3–9). Apart from his normal duties, Behr was quite a popular pianist and accomplished songwriter, having composed the 509th's unofficial theme song, "Silver Wings." This composition exhibited such flair that it was recorded by baritone and movie star Nelson Eddy and also by popular musician Meredith Willson. The song enjoyed frequent airing on Armed Forces Radio.

With crew and bomb aboard, Tibbets waved from the cockpit (3–10). Poised for an encounter with destiny such as few men experience, *Enola Gay* and her crew prepared to taxi out of the hardstand and onto the runway (3–11 and 3–12). The plane took off at two A.M. sharp.

Dozens of cameramen still lined the runway "to record our departure for the archives of the Manhattan Project and for history itself," as Tibbets put it. The plane lifted smoothly and climbed to cruising altitude of some 8,000 feet. At this point Captain Parsons and Lieutenant Jeppson moved to the bomb bay to arm the bomb. In about twenty minutes they advised Tibbets that the task was done, and the pilot so informed Tinian.

3-10 Tibbets waves from the cockpit of *Enola Gay* just prior to takeoff.

3-11

3-12 *Enola Gay* prepared to taxi onto the runway at North Field, Tinian.

At daybreak the *Enola Gay* rendezvoused with the two escort planes, which had been circling over Iwo Jima. Then Tibbets activated the automatic pilot and turned the B-29 over to copilot Captain Robert A. Lewis. Moving to the rear of the aircraft, Tibbets briefed his crew concerning exactly what they were going to do. When the plane was some forty minutes off the coast of Japan, word came in from Eatherly that Hiroshima offered "clear skies with unlimited visibility." They could forget about alternate targets, so Dutch Van Kirk immediately gave Tibbets the heading for Hiroshima.

Situated on Honshu some hundred miles northeast of the Strait of Shimonoseki (3–13), Hiroshima had begun in the 1500s as a town huddled around the castle of the area's feudal lord, Terumoto Mori. It was located on new delta land deposited by the Ota River, and during the "Edo era," or Tokugawa shogunate (1603–1867), the inhabitants cleared and created new land to extend their town. As the city grew, its character was molded by its many islands, connected by a complex of bridges (3–14).

During the reign of the great emperor Meiji (1867–1912), Hiroshima became closely affiliated with

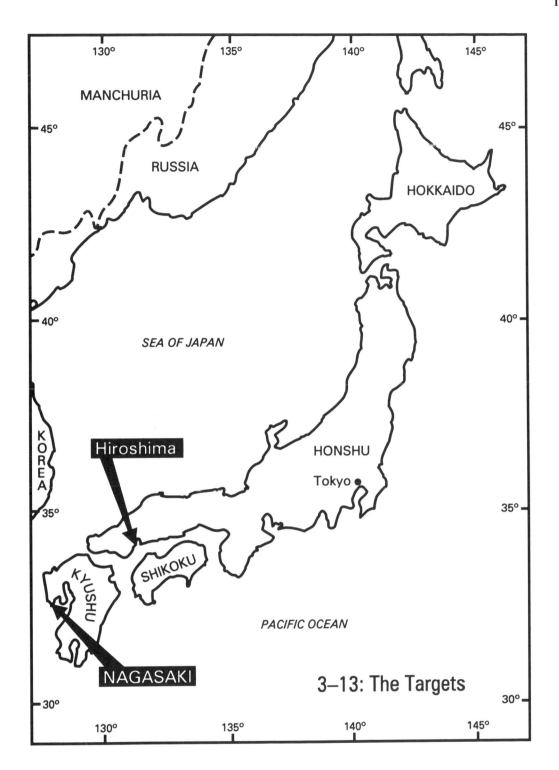

3–13: The Targets

the armed forces. Located as it was on the shore of the Inland Sea, it served as a base for troops headed overseas to fight in the Sino-Japanese and Russo-Japanese wars. Nearby was the major naval base at Kure.

By 1945, the city ranked as Japan's seventh-largest, with a population of roughly 350,000. Its industrial complex, although not so extensive as that of some other Japanese cities of similar size, was closely related to the military (3–15). The Hiroshima plant of the Japan Steel Company was a major source of heavy arms. Toyo Industry and Mitsubishi Electric Manufacturing Company produced precision tools and machinery, while lesser plants turned out such items as aircraft parts, chemicals, and food.

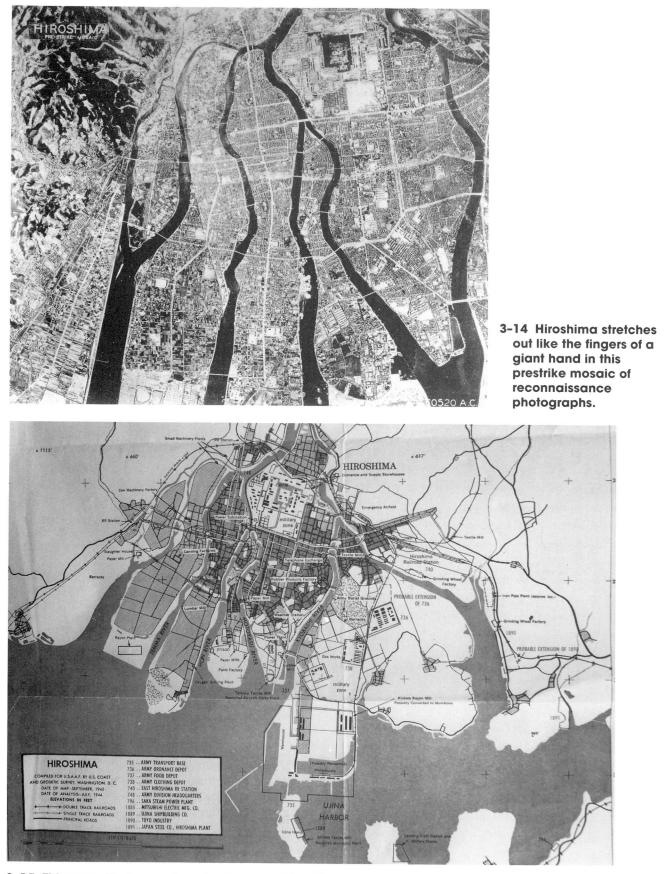

3-14 Hiroshima stretches out like the fingers of a giant hand in this prestrike mosaic of reconnaissance photographs.

3-15 This map displays various features marking Hiroshima as a legitimate military target.

3-16 During the Sino-Japanese War, Emperor Meiji made his headquarters in this building.

3-17 Ujima Harbor, developed as a port for Hiroshima, was a major point of embarkation for the Japanese Army.

Hiroshima was headquarters of the Second Army Group, under the command of Marshal Shunroku Hata. Hata's headquarters were in the same building within the old Imperial castle grounds that Emperor Meiji had used during the Sino-Japanese War (3–16).

Japan had only two marshals, so Hata's presence testified to the importance of his mission and his headquarters. Hata was expected to head the all-out defense of Kyushu—across the Inland Sea from Hiroshima—against the American invasion of that island, anticipated to begin some time in the early autumn of 1945.

The eastern and northeastern sides of Hiroshima had been declared military zones. Hata's headquarters, with various administration buildings, barracks, and storage, stood north of the city's center. Just across the Kyobashi River were located army ordnance, clothing, and food depots.

Ujima Harbor, a principal embarkation point, was home to the army transport base. The main anchorages were off nearby Ujima Island, and the island itself housed a repair yard. The port was a major communications and trade center, servicing passenger liners from Shikoku and Ujima (3–17).

Hiroshima in 1945 presented, in general, a picture of comfortable middle-class urban living. It had its share of museums, beautifully landscaped gardens, and temples

3-18 View looking northeast down Tera-machi, the Street of Temples. The road here was considerably wider than in most of the residential areas. No buildings in this area survived.

3-19 Aerial view of the very densely built-up area of the city on the Motoyasu River looking upstream.

(3-18). A 1941 guidebook for Japan credited the city with being a center for the production of such items as paper umbrellas, seaweed, oysters, lemons, and persimmons.

Like all modern cities, Hiroshima had a number of heavily congested areas such as the one portrayed in photo 3-19. Except for very heavy masonry structures, this entire area would be devastated in the strike. Ground zero for the bmb was upper right in the photo, opposite the second bend in the river. Even closer to ground zero was the City Commercial Display Building (3-20). Another prominent landmark near ground zero was the T-Bridge that linked the city's eastern, western, and southern areas (3-21).

A primary communications medium was radio station JOFK (3-22), one of the few domestic stations in Japan

3-20 An early photograph looking upstream on the Motoyasu River toward what would become the most famous of all Hiroshima landmarks—the domed City Commercial Display Building, immediately adjacent to ground zero.

3-21 An older photo looking north from the vicinity of the T-Bridge.

3-22 Radio station JOFK. This main building housed studios, offices, and transmitters.

3-23 View looking east into Hiroshima's shopping district.

3-24 The living room in an upper-middle-class Hiroshima home.

operating at 10,000 watts. A secondary transmitter was located five kilometers north of the city, connected by a cable.

Unfortunately, much of Hiroshima was one large fire-trap. Even in the bustling shopping district (3–23), equivalent to Tokyo's famed Ginza, many wooden structures still stood. Much of Hiroshima's domestic architecture, although charming, was highly inflammable. Photo 3–24 shows the living room of an upper-middle-class Hiroshima home, its decor typical of the period. Likenesses of the Emperor and Empress attest to the owners' loyalty. The cabinet at center contains a Buddhist image. Dolls and wall hangings (kakemono) were popular items of decoration. The hibachi, or charcoal brazier, in the

lower portion of the photograph, was the sole source of heat in most dwellings.

Photo 3–25, of another living room, features straw mats (tatami), almost a necessity in a well-to-do Japanese home. Its proud possessor described the kitchen shown in photo 3–26 as "modern." The unit consists of a masonry firebox with two grated openings in the top. Charcoal was placed in the stoves, ignited, and fanned to provide heat for cooking.

Such interior features were quite enough to ensure ever-present fire hazards, but the actual construction of such homes was an open invitation to disaster. The workers in photo 3–27 are mixing straw into the plaster for a house's exterior walls. The lathing is split bamboo.

3-25 Another living room, showing straw mats (tatami) and low table (*dai*).

3-26 A Hiroshima kitchen, which its owner described as modern.

3-27 This view of a house under construction shows workers mixing straw into the plaster for this house's exterior walls. Note the split-bamboo lathing.

3–28 The plaster-and-bamboo lathing typical of exterior walls in Japanese domestic architecture.

Photo 3–28 reveals how damage to a typical Hiroshima home has exposed to public view the architectural features that caused buildings in Japanese cities to go up in smoke by the hundreds of thousands during the Twentieth Air Force's massive firebomb raids.

One can easily understand why fire for centuries had been Japan's number one nightmare, and why the popular expression "a thief at a fire," meaning one who enriches himself as a result of a neighbor's misfortune, carried such a connotation of contempt.

In spite of the "clear and present danger," all too much of Japan's firefighting equipment was hopelessly inadequate. Photos 3–29 and 3–30 picture hand-drawn water pumpers, typical of the outdated technology serving many Japanese cities, including Hiroshima. Two young women firefighters demonstrate in photo 3–31 the motive power required to move their equipment. Presumably they were supposed to be ready for action, but the very thin slip-on cloth boots, thonged between the first and second toes, would offer less than no protection if these women had to enter a burning building. These survive to the present day as the standard Japanese work shoes.

By war's end, modern buildings had begun to replace Hiroshima's older wooden structures. But that was too late to be of any help in August 1945, when the firestorm caused by the atomic bomb would kill or main at least as many victims as the blast itself.

3–29 A hand-drawn water pumper.

3-30 Another smaller pumper.

3-31 Two young female firefighters demonstrate movement of their equipment.

CHAPTER 4

The Hiroshima Bomb

Breaking radio silence, which was no longer important, Tibbets informed the escort planes that *Enola Gay* was on her final course. Five minutes away from the target, Tom Ferebee began the countdown (4–1). At the one-minute point, Tibbets ordered the escorts to drop back, and all aboard *Enola Gay* put on thick black glasses. The plane leaped upward with the release of the heavy bomb (4–2), and Tibbets banked sharply to put as much distance as possible between the plane and the explosion. He estimated that in the fifty-one seconds between release and explosion, the B-29's altitude of some 33,000 feet, plus the distance gained by banking, would put it ten miles from the drop site. During those fifty-one seconds Tibbets found himself wondering if "the gadget" really would work.

Hiroshima had experienced two air-raid warnings that morning. At 12:25 A.M. a red alert warned of an enemy plane overhead; this alert was canceled at 2:10. Then, at 7:09, came a yellow alert that enemy planes were nearing—probably triggered by the *Straight Flush*; this warning was cleared at 7:31. The three bomb planes were spotted, and the following yellow-alert message was prepared:

4-1 This annotated aerial photograph, taken August 8, 1945, shows Major Ferebee's aiming point and various landmarks within the city.

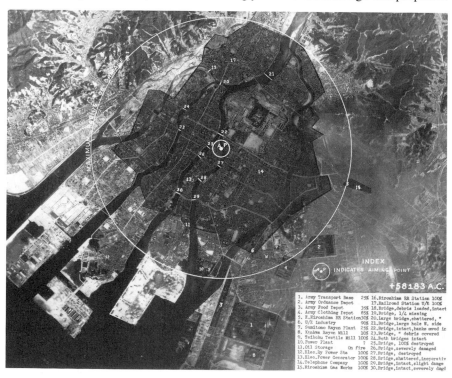

4-2 Little Boy, the Hiroshima bomb that Major Ferebee toggled out of *Enola Gay* at 8:15 A.M. Hiroshima time on August 6, 1945.

"Chugokyu District Army Information at 8:13 A.M.: three enemy Superfortresses proceeding westward over Saijo area. Strict precautions should be taken." But the bomb exploded at 8:15 A.M. Hiroshima time, before the warning could go into effect, so Hiroshima was going about its early-morning business as usual (4–3). Many citizens of the city, and others from nearby towns, including some 8,000 schoolchildren aged thirteen and fourteen, were working at demolishing buildings to provide fire escape routes for use in case of air raids.

The bomb exploded at about 1,740 feet above the Shima Surgical Hospital, which stood some 900 feet southeast of the important T-shaped Aioi Bridge (4–4). The burst temperature was estimated to reach over a million degrees Celsius. This ignited the surrounding air, which formed a fireball some 840 feet in diameter (4–5). To eyewitnesses five and a half miles away, its bright-

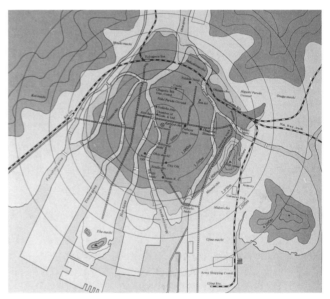

4-3 Map of Hiroshima, showing ground zero and the city's geographical features.

4-4 Far end of the T-Bridge. The buckled brickwork and misaligned trolley tracks attest that the structure was moved over approximately one foot to the right.

4–5 A fiery cloud boils skyward from Hiroshima at about 8:18.

4–6 Ten to twenty minutes after the detonation, a mushroom cloud stands over Hiroshima, leveled out at about 60,000 feet by the stratosphere inversion.

ness exceeded the sun tenfold. In *Enola Gay,* tail gunner Staff Sergeant George C. Caron, facing ground zero, saw the light through his dark glasses and closed eyelids. Two shock waves hit the aircraft, the first with a force of at least two Gs, just as the scientists had predicted; the second was noticeably weaker. Tibbets banked the aircraft back toward the city to assess results. As he did so, those aboard saw an awesome spectacle—the enormous mushroom-shaped cloud that was to become the best-known image of the attack (4–6).

Within a radius of one kilometer from the hypocenter, most of the victims died on August 6 or a few days later from burns and ruptured internal organs (4–7). Serious burns also afflicted a great many people (4–8), but results tapered off at the three-kilometer mark to "comparatively light" skin burns. Many people's clothing was either burned away or literally blown off by the blast (4–9 and 4–10). Map 4–11 identifies locations of all subsequent aerial photographs.

4-7 The last halting steps of an unknown Hiroshima inhabitant.

4-8 This young soldier's face was burned when he looked toward the explosion: his cap protected the top of his head.

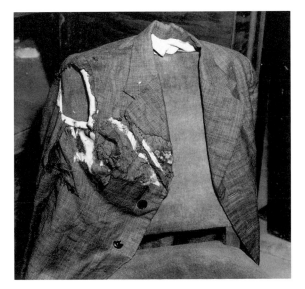

4-9, 4-10 Tattered clothing recovered from bomb victims after the explosion.

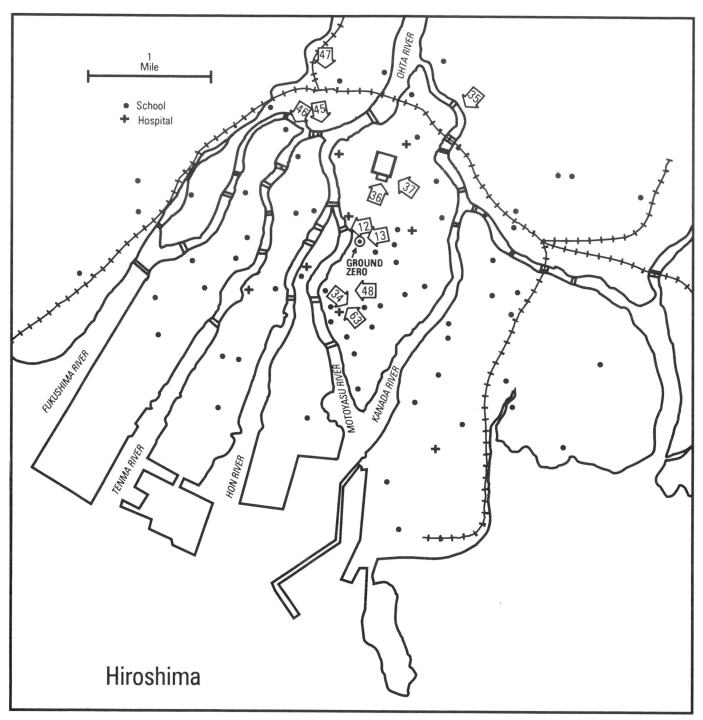

4-11

In addition to those killed as a direct result of the explosion, thousands perished as wooden houses to a radius of 2.6 kilometers were either totally destroyed or damaged beyond repair (4–12). Understandably, casualty figures could only be estimates, and indeed have never been finalized. Soon after the attack the Japanese reported 71,379 dead or missing and 68,023 injured, 19,691 of them seriously. Of 24,158 soldiers stationed in Hiroshima, 6,769 were killed.

Concrete buildings (4–13 and 4–14) fared little better than those made of wood: Ceilings came crashing down, doors and windows blew away, and fittings were destroyed (4–15). Outside a one-kilometer radius, the concrete structures withstood the initial shock (4–16), but their interiors were a prey to fires that raged throughout the city and burned everything combustible within a two-kilometer circle. The shock wave that rocked *Enola Gay* contributed heavily to the damage as it struck everything

4-12 Looking toward the city center from directly over ground zero. Note the absence of rubble above ground level, the wooden structures having been reduced to ashes.

4-13 Ground zero at Hiroshima (indicated by the arrow), looking east. Only reinforced-concrete buildings remain and all have sustained significant structural damage. The T- Bridge and the City Commercial Display Building, both ground zero landmarks, are visible in the upper portion.

4-14 Near ground zero, masonry or brick structures failed to stand up to the blast.

4-15 The searing heat of the explosion manifested itself even inside buildings. Here, a window's outline is scorched onto three chairs.

4-16 This view of Hiroshima reveals the extent of damage. Not until 1¹/₄ miles from ground zero are structures standing without apparent damage, even seen from this relatively high altitude.

on the surface, then rebounded with a force that even a mile and a half from the hypocenter was estimated at 135 feet per second.

A strange phenomenon of shadowing, or ghosting, was an eerie aspect of the bombing. This occurred when certain objects shielded others from heat and radiation. Supporting latticework for a gas storage tank produced the effect seen in photo 4–17. The image of a ladder burned into the same tank attests to the intensity of the heat and radiation the bomb generated (4–18). In photo 4–19, the shadow of a valve and hand wheel indicates the direction of the blast. One of Hiroshima's many bridges displays the ghostly outline of handrails (4–20). Even human beings vaporized by intense heat left behind shadowy evidence when they briefly masked the pavement beside them, as on the bridge seen in photo 4–20 (4- 21).

4-17 An example of the ghosting phenomenon. Lattice at a gas storage tank produced the effect seen here.

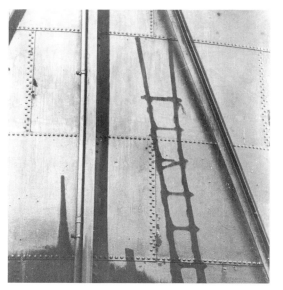

4-18 The shadow of a ladder seared into the same gas storage tank bears witness to the intensity of the heat and radiation from the bomb explosion.

4-19 The image produced by a valve and hand wheel documents the precise direction of the radiation/heat source.

4-20 Ghostly outlines of guard rails on one of Hiroshima's many bridges.

4-21 Human beings vaporized by the intense heat left ghostly traces of their last moments.

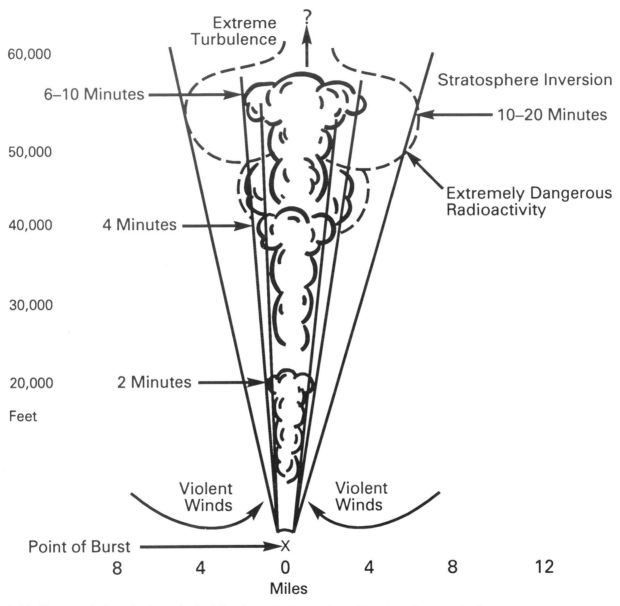

4–22 The most dreaded symbol of the twentieth century. The development of a mushroom cloud, as analyzed by the U.S. Strategic Bombing Survey.

From his height of 33,000 feet, and keeping a cautious distance from the mushroom cloud (4–22), Tibbets could not see the details of what had happened, and would not fully comprehend it until he studied the photographs several days later. But he and his crew could see enough to realize that the destruction surpassed their wildest imaginings. In fact, none of the prearranged code messages fit the situation. Deciding that in the circumstances caution was pointless, Tibbets informed Tinian in the clear that results exceeded all predictions. Then he slept for four

hours—the first time in his flying career that he had been able to sleep in an aircraft (4–23).

At Tinian what looked to the men like the entire population of the island had turned out (4–24). Generals Spaatz and LeMay had flown in from Guam. Spaatz pinned the Distinguished Service Cross on Tibbets's chest (4–25 and 4–26); then the generals bore the fliers off for a half-hour's close debriefing by a star-studded group (4–27 and 4–28). Finally, LeMay let them off the

4-23 *Enola Gay* returns to Tinian on August 6.

4-24 An excited crowd of 509th Composite Group personnel huddles close to *Enola Gay.*

4-25 General Spaatz greets Colonel Tibbets and awards him the Distinguished Service Cross.

4-26 Spaatz returns Tibbets's salute, as Brigadier General John H. Davies, commander of the 313th Bombardment Wing, looks on.

4-27 Immediately following the decoration ceremony on the hardstand, Tibbets's men were debriefed by a stellar assembly, including (l-r): Rear Admiral Purnell, General Spaatz, Lieutenant General Barney M. Giles (Spaatz's deputy commander), and Lieutenant General Twining, shown here waiting for the debriefing to commence.

4-28 An unidentified officer questions Tibbets's navigator, Captain Van Kirk. Others seated at the table (clockwise from Van Kirk) are: Colonel Tibbets, Rear Admiral Purnell, Lieutenant General Twining, Lieutenant General Giles, General Spaatz, Captain Parsons, Lieutenant Beser, Major Ferebee, and Brooklyn Dodger fan Staff Sergeant Caron. Brigadier General Davies looks on from behind and to the right of General Giles.

4-29 A large assemblage of 509th personnel attended the ceremony held on August 9 to honor Tibbets's men.

4-30 Members of Tibbets's crew were decorated by Brigadier General Davies. Present at the ceremony are (l-r): Colonel Tibbets, Captain Parsons, Brigadier General Davies, Captain Lewis (face hidden), Lieutenant Beser, Lieutenant Jeppson, Staff Sergeant Duzenbury, Staff Sergeant Caron, Sergeant Stiborik, Sergeant Shumard, Private First Class Nelson.

hook: "Kids, go eat, take a good shower, and sleep as much as you want!"

Another ceremony to honor Tibbets's men took place on August 9 (4–29 and 4–30), oddly enough the same day as the Nagasaki strike, when one would have expected all attention to be focused on Sweeney and his crews. But Tibbets had been first, and from the start the Hiroshima mission overshadowed Nagasaki.

Within five hours of the Hiroshima strike, F-13s overflew the city to assess results (4–31). Obviously, the bomb's effects were immense, but the vast quantity of fire, smoke, and dust made it impossible to estimate accurately the degree of damage the city had suffered. As of August 11, the total area destroyed and damaged was estimated at 4.7 square miles, or 68.5 percent of the city. Among specific targets, the army food depot was 25 percent damaged; Teikoku Textile Mill 100 percent damaged; Signal Corps, 2nd Company, 12 percent destroyed, 55 percent damaged (4–32); unidentified industry, 50 percent damaged, 50 percent destroyed (4–33). The East

4-31 Boeing F-13 reconnaissance aircraft, which was a B-29 modified to carry photographic equipment.

4-32 Japanese army barracks 4,200 feet north of ground zero, close by the old castle complex. Partly because of the blast pressure from the outside, and partly because of debris from collapsed roofs and floors, masonry and brickwork were blasted into the interiors of structures, rather than flying outward in the pattern associated with hits sustained during conventional bombing.

4-33 Hiroshima's war industries located away from the city center naturally suffered less, but still sustained considerable damage such as that seen in the munitions plant here.

4-34 Hiroshima railroad station.

Hiroshima Railroad Station and Yards received only minor damage (4–34), but Army division headquarters was 100 percent destroyed (4–35). Curiously, in photo 4–36 small structures at the lower edge of the moat appear intact. Perhaps these had been erected since the blast. What seem to be small tents are set up at lower left. Some trees in the compound still stood, as well as others along the riverbank (4–37).

Communications between Hiroshima and higher military and naval headquarters had been severed, so initial news that something frightful had occurred at Hiroshima came from nearby towns. As those reporting had no idea of what had happened beyond an enormous explosion and a sinister cloud, these first bits and pieces aroused more puzzlement than alarm. At the navy's underground headquarters at Kasumigazeki in Tokyo, the navy's homeland air defense officer, Commander Masatake Okumiya, received one such message from Kure at about 8:30 A.M. The caller described "a terrible flash" and "a terrible mushroom-like cloud" and "a heavy roar." Obviously "something big" had happened. But what? Okumiya wondered. Only a few enemy aircraft had been reported over Hiroshima. Perhaps an ammunition dump had exploded, but he did not know whether the army had any such facility at Hiroshima. He could find out nothing at headquarters, even though he thought the problem serious enough to break into a meeting of the naval general staff. The admirals neither knew nor, apparently, cared. The report was vague, Hiroshima was an army town, and the navy had more than enough on its own plate.

Still uneasy, Okumiya called Captain Yasukado Yasui at the Naval Bureau of Aeronautics, and told him what he had heard from Kure. Yasui's suggestion that this

4-35 Ruins of the old Imperial Castle and army headquarters compound at center, half a mile from ground zero, looking southwest.

4-36 Imperial Castle and army headquarters compound. This photo is undated.

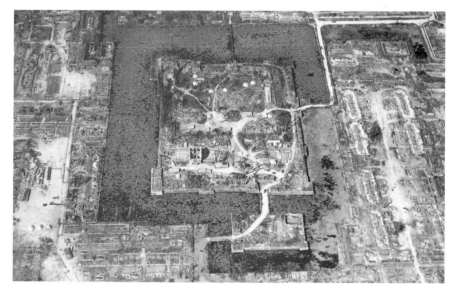

4-37 Looking west past the castle compound.

4–38 Captain Mitsuo Fuchida, air operations officer of the Japanese navy. As a commander, he had led the air attack on Pearl Harbor.

4–39 Marquis Koichi Kido, Lord Keeper of the Privy Seal.

4–40 Dr. Yoshio Nishina, Japanese authority on atomic energy.

might be an atomic explosion shocked Okumiya. He knew that both the army and navy had been working on the possibility, but as far as he knew the project had not gone beyond "scientific investigation." Could the Americans have succeeded?

Okumiya's longtime friend, Captain Mitsuo Fuchida (4–38), the navy's air operations officer, received word of the virtual destruction of Hiroshima from Navy Chief of Staff Admiral Shikazo Yano. For a few minutes he was utterly stunned, because he himself had been in Hiroshima attending an army conference until late the previous afternoon. From Yano's description, however, he had no doubt what had happened. "This must be the atomic bomb," he told Yano. And he urged the admiral to pressure the naval general staff to act at once to secure peace.

Far up the chain of command, Emperor Hirohito was of the same opinion. Immediately after the attack, His Majesty received the Lord Keeper of the Privy Seal, Marquis Koichi Kido (4–39). Kido found that "the reports of the indescribably tragic conditions" had left the Emperor "overwhelmed with grief." And he commanded, "Under the circumstances, we must bow to the inevitable. No matter what happens to my safety, we must put an end to this war as speedily as possible so that this tragedy will not be repeated."

Not everyone was as realistic or as concerned with the Japanese people's welfare as Hirohito was. There was a strong disinclination to believe that what had happened was truly an atomic explosion, even after Truman's official announcement:

Sixteen hours ago an American airplane dropped one bomb on Hiroshima. . . . It is an atomic bomb . . . . We are now prepared to obliterate more rapidly and completely every

productive enterprise the Japanese have above ground in any city. . . . If they do not now accept our terms they may expect a rain of ruin from the air the like of which has never been seen on this earth.

Perhaps inevitably, the initial Japanese reaction was to form a committee. The "Atomic Bomb Countermeasure Committee" was established in the cabinet with Sumihisa Ikeda, chief of the cabinet planning bureau, as chairman. Members came from the War, Navy, and Home ministries and included Technical Board representatives. At the first meeting, held on August 7, these latter members "strongly insisted that the bomb was not an atomic bomb." They claimed that "no matter how advanced American technique may be" it was impossible for the Americans to have brought "such unstable weapons as atomic devices to Japan, across the Pacific." They added, "We do not know what will happen in the future, but to date American technique is not that highly developed."

In some asperity, Ikeda reminded them of Truman's statement. "I can hardly imagine that the Americans would broadcast such a lie. If it is not an atomic bomb, what is it?" And the technicians declared, "It must be a new type [of] bomb with special equipment, but its content is unknown." As a result, the word "atomic" did not appear in the initial public announcement.

Meanwhile, both the army and navy had sent teams to investigate the site. The army's group included Dr. Yoshio Nishina (4–40), Japan's "highest authority on atomic energy." He noted that "the general opinion in the military circles" was that Truman's announcement was probably "propaganda to scare the Japanese." So at the time Nishina withheld judgment, but his first aerial view of Hiroshima convinced him that "it definitely was the work of an atomic bomb" (4–41, 4–42, and 4–43).

4-41 Hiroshima from high altitude, August 7, 1945, exhibits few details, except for its roadnet.

4-42, 4-43 Two photographs offered as a comparison in the Strategic Bombing Survey study of Hiroshima, one before and one after the bomb explosion, showing the City Commercial Display Building.

4–44 Five overlapping photographs provide a stark, wide-angle view of Hiroshima from the vicinity of ground zero (indicated by the arrow). The City Commercial Display Building is at center. At right is the T-Bridge, near the divergence of the Matoyan and Ota rivers.

Fuchida and Okumiya were among those who hurried to the scene. Both men had spent years in the thick of aerial combat and were no strangers to horror, but what they saw was beyond all experience and all ability of words to convey. "It was like an evil nightmare," recalled Fuchida. Indeed, the contrast between these grotesque ruins and the pleasant city where only two days ago he had been conferring with fellow officers must have been overwhelming.

The familiar T-Bridge's barriers had been knocked

4–45 Ground zero at Hiroshima (indicated by the arrow), looking south.

outward; utility poles stood at various angles, blown out by the blast (which had pushed aside countless tons of air), then pulled back by the suction created as air was forced back into the partial vacuum. Rainwater had collected in a pool on the roof of a building at the foot of the bridge, pushed down by the force of the blast (4–44).

Looking across the city, Fuchida, Okumiya, and the other investigators could see that many familiar landmarks no longer existed, or were changed almost beyond recognition (4–45, 4–46, and 4–47). It was all too easy to see the devastation, which near ground zero was almost total (4–48, 4–49, and 4–50), because the inspectors had

4-46 View of the island straddled by the Tenma and Fukushima rivers. The tip of the island is at lower right.

4-47 Looking south toward the ground zero area from a point ³/₄ mile farther north.

to proceed on foot. Transportation had come to an abrupt halt, streets were congested with refugees, and, while many bridges had survived, others did not (4–51).

Within half a mile of ground zero, even the strongest modern structures had suffered significant damage (4–52). At about 800 feet south of the hypocenter, the blast had crushed a corner of the Hiroshima Gas Company's building (4–53 and 4–54). Of the Koa Fire Insur-

4-48 View looking west across the breadth of the city, half a mile from ground zero.

4-49, 4-50 View of the ruined city from atop the Red Cross building, half a mile from ground zero.

4-51 Although many of Hiroshima's bridges survived the explosion, some lighter ones did not.

4-52 Modern structures within half a mile of ground zero suffered severe damage, most often in the form of walls buckled away from the direction of the explosion.

4-53, 4-54 Hiroshima Gas Company, 800 feet south of ground zero. This structure also appears along the far left edge of 4-50. The City Commercial Display Building stands at far right in the first photo of this pair.

4-55 Koa Fire Insurance Company, 1,300 feet from ground zero. Brick buildings did not fare as well as those of concrete and steel.

ance Company's headquarters, located 1,300 feet from ground zero, little remained but the vault (4–55). Photos 4–56 and 4–57 give a before-and-after view of the Chugokyu Electric Company's Minami substation, 1,500 feet from the hypocenter.

A little farther along, in the 2,000-foot radius, the Shimomuna Watch Shop had been pushed off its foundations and listed at a 10-degree angle (4–58). Five hundred feet farther from ground zero, the Hiroshima Telephone Company's switch and relay rack room was destroyed (4–59), mute evidence of why the news of the

4-56, 4-57 Chugokyu Electric Company's Minami substation, before and after the bombing, 1,500 feet from ground zero.

4-58 Shimomuna Watch Shop, a steel-frame building, 2,000 feet from ground zero.

4-59 Hiroshima Telephone Company, 2,500 feet from ground zero. Here, the switch and relay rack room lies destroyed. This picture was taken on October 28, 1945.

disaster did not get through immediately. At 3,000 feet, Hiroshima's city hall had been gutted by fire (4–60). Incredibly, this city with so much wooden construction had only one hook-and-ladder truck, and it was destroyed (4–61).

As usual in disasters, there were some freakish survivals. The earth-and-log air-raid shelter pictured in photo 4–62 survived intact, although neighboring buildings succumbed. Photo 4–63 shows the Hiroshima Red Cross Hospital, about one mile from ground zero. Some buildings stood and considerably more heaped rubble remained at this distance.

Beyond the one-and-a-half-mile boundary, some wooden structures remained, albeit badly damaged (4–64). Many steel and concrete buildings appeared intact at first glance, but their outer walls hid internal damage of the type associated with the downward pressure of the air burst (4–65, 4–66, and 4–67). At the Chugokyu

4-60 Hiroshima's forlorn city hall stands empty, gutted by fire, some 3,000 feet from the hypocenter. This photo was taken on November 1, 1945.

4-61 At a branch of the Hiroshima Fire Department, the city's only hook-and-ladder truck lies charred alongside two other vehicles, 4,000 feet from ground zero.

4–62 The earth-and-log air-raid shelter at center survived the blast intact 5,000 feet northeast of ground zero, although other buildings did not.

4–63 Farther south, looking northwest. Hiroshima Red Cross Hospital lies at center near the river, about one mile from ground zero.

4–64 Beyond 1½ miles from ground zero, some wooden buildings, such as this one 7,600 feet away, survived, although badly buckled and knocked about.

4–65, 4–66, 4–67 At the Misawa Credit Association Warehouse, the walls stand but the ceiling and the entire second floor have been pushed down to ground level. Where the ceilings have held, they appear as if battered by a demolition ball.

Power Company's offices, the blast carried away portions of the building's downspouts (4–68). A reinforced concrete smokestack had fallen, and at a little distance a power pole canted in the opposite direction, pushed by the blast and then sucked back by air rushing into the partial vacuum (4–69). The Commercial Display Building and its annex were still prominent features. Even a few nearby trees still stood (4–70, 4–71, and 4–72). The streets, too, had suffered damage, perhaps in part from collapsed storm drains or sewers (4–73). One thing was

4–68 The blast carried away portions of the Chugokyu Power Company's downspouts.

4–69 A reinforced concrete smokestack lies on its side. Note the power pole in the distance leaning in the opposite direction.

4–70 Near the Commercial Display Building, trees still stand at right with branches charred, but intact.

4–71 The rubble-strewn courtyard of the Commercial Display Building. Unfortunately, the text on the board bound to the concrete post at lower right is illegible.

4–72 The annex adjacent to the Commercial Display Building.

4-73 A Hiroshima street. Note the drainpipe, which the vacuum created by the atomic blast has pulled up through the pavement.

4-74 A cemetery in disarray, possibly the army burial grounds about 1$\frac{1}{4}$ miles from ground zero. The only legible stone, that of army captain Akira Sasaki, is at lower right.

abundantly clear: If Hiroshima was to arise again, the mammoth task of rebuilding would start literally from the ground up.

Even the dead had been disturbed, as evidenced by photo 4–74 of a cemetery. This was probably the Army Burial Grounds on the east bank of the Kyobashi River. Among the casualties was a Christian church (4–75, 4–76, and 4–77). Many years later, when Fuchida visited Hiroshima as a Christian evangelist, he met a pastor who had clung to a picture of the ruins of his former church—probably this very edifice. Fuchida persuaded him to get rid of it, turn his back on the past, and devote himself to his new church and flock.

For both Fuchida and Okumiya, their memories centered on people rather than property, however horrifying

the destruction. In later days Fuchida could not allow himself to go too deeply into details. He particularly remembered the bodies piled higher than his head along the rivers and canals. Burn victims had sought cooling water, but the water was hot, and thousands died on the banks. Fuchida never forgot the pall that covered much of the city from a "black rain" that had fallen within about half an hour of the explosion—a rain made black by mud, dust, and soot that swirled upward.

Okumiya's account was more graphic, although he knew that neither words nor film could convey the horrible actuality—the screams of the dying, the "dust and ash swirling around the burned bodies," the stench of burning flesh, survivors placing the dead and dying in long rows of mats and planks.

4-75, 4-76, 4-77 Christianity was (and remains) very much a minority religion in Japan. Ruins of churches in Japan seem to have been of particular interest to Americans. This particular church caught the eye of at least three different photographers—one each from the U.S. Army Air Forces, the U.S. Strategic Bombing Survey (USSBS), and the U.S. Navy.

A rumor began circulating that a second atomic bomb had landed nearby but had not exploded. Fuchida got together with Captain Yasui, a boyhood schoolmate, to search Hiroshima's outskirts. A few miles north of the city they came upon a parachute. Approaching a few steps at a time, they found attached to it a cylinder, which Fuchida opened gingerly. It contained several instruments, including a thermometer, a timing device, and a radio—obviously to record and send back to the Americans technical information about the bomb drop.

Lieutenant General Seizo Arisue, chief of the intelligence bureau of Imperial General Headquarters, Army Section, headed the army's investigative team. As his plane approached Hiroshima, he could see that it "assumed an entirely different appearance from other bombed cities . . . . I intuitively realized that an unconventional type of bomb had been used." At the airfield an officer met them. One side of his face had been burned, but not the other. This officer explained, "Everything which is exposed gets burnt, but anything which is covered even slightly can escape burns. Therefore it cannot be said that there are no countermeasures."

Evidently this flicker of hope impressed Arisue. Writing by candlelight from the Ujima Shipping Command, he reported to Tokyo: "1. A special bomb was used. 2. Burns can be prevented by covering the body. 3. Rumor has it that the same kind of bomb will be dropped on Tokyo on 12 August." Obviously Arisue still could not bring himself to use the word "atomic."

Another high-ranking officer inclined to clutch at straws was Admiral Soemu Toyoda, chief of the naval general staff (4–78). The news that the United States had perfected and used the atomic bomb "was quite a shock" to him.

However, I personally had doubts as to whether the American forces would continue to drop atom bombs at frequent intervals . . . . I did not know what the principal composition of an atom bomb was but I was certain that it was a radioactive element. It was my opinion that all the radium-like elements in the world could not have amounted to much.

Therefore Toyoda doubted that the United States could produce the huge quantity needed; he "believed that the number of atom bombs which could be used in a given time was greatly restricted and that this number definitely would not be great."

He also believed that the Americans would not continue to drop atomic bombs "because of the criticism from the standpoint of laws of war and ethics . . . . I wondered whether the world would permit the United States to continue such an inhuman atrocity." Perhaps the Americans themselves would not consent to further atomic warfare.

It is barely possible that Toyoda did not know that the Japanese had worked hard to develop the atomic bomb, and certainly would have had no compunction about using it had they succeeded. In mid-1941 the navy had instituted a top-priority program to that end, with Nishina in charge. Although fully aware of the difficulties, Nishina and his colleagues considered it worth trying. But after about a year the project had to be abandoned as beyond Japan's capability at the time.

Later Lieutenant General Torashiro Kawabe, as assistant chief of the army aeronautical department, assigned "several young technical officers" to work with Nishina at the Physical and Chemical Institute. On "one chilly day" in late 1941 he visited the institute, where he "received the impression that the research was in an embryo

4–78 Admiral Soemu Toyoda (left), navy chief of staff, examines a chart at the headquarters of the Imperial Combined Fleet in April 1944. On the right sits Captain Mitsuo Fuchida.

stage." In contrast, someone informed him that in the United States "research on atomic energy seemed to be in an advanced stage." In June 1945, after Kawabe had become assistant chief of the army general staff, he "received a report that the research work on atomic energy by Dr. Nishina would be temporarily suspended. This was because the very critical war situation made it necessary that we concentrate all endeavors on the imminent decisive battle for the homeland, while the research in atomic energy was still far from a final success."

Nishina attributed Japan's lag in atomic research to four points: the small number of qualified scientists; the limited funds for such research; the fact that Japan had insufficient industrial capacity to turn theory into reality; lack of the necessary uranium ore. He also believed that, unlike the United States, Japan under wartime conditions had neither the organization nor the leadership to mobilize its scientists. And the loss of his own laboratory during an air raid in April 1945 was a severe blow, as was the army aeronautical department's move out of Tokyo, which made close liaison impossible.

This failure may help explain the reluctance of Japan's armed forces to admit that the bomb was truly atomic. Foreign Minister Shigenori Togo (4–79) had to deal with this psychology on August 7 at a meeting of cabinet ministers. "The Army tried to minimize the effect of the bomb by repeating that we were not sure that an atom bomb had been used and insisted that we wait for the investigation reports." Togo had no such trouble the next morning in audience with the Emperor. His Majesty "indicated clearly that the enemy's new weapon made it impossible to go on fighting." He commanded Togo "to end the war immediately" and "to convey his wishes to the Premier."

CHAPTER 5

The Nagasaki Bomb

The ninth of August was what Togo with commendable restraint called "a bad day." First came word that the Soviet Union had declared war on Japan, after which, Ikeda believed, Japan's "chances were gone." The once-mighty Kwantung Army in Manchuria "was no more than a hollow shell," having been drained since late 1944 to bolster Japan's defenses "in preparation for the decisive battle on the homeland."

Togo "had to fight all day," first at the Supreme Council for Direction of the War, then at a cabinet meeting, and finally at an Imperial Conference in the evening. It was during the meeting of the Supreme War Council that the members received word of the bombing of Nagasaki—an event that seems to have had no appreciable effect on the discussions held that day.

The pattern of preparations for the second atomic mission closely followed the first. The general plan was the same, although choice of targets was limited to two—first choice Kokura, second Nagasaki. This time the strike aircraft was *Bock's Car,* although not under its usual pilot, Captain Frederick C. Bock. *The Great Artiste,* Sweeney's B-29, was still loaded with scientific instruments from the Hiroshima mission, so it was decided that once again it would serve as a support plane while Sweeney and his crew took over *Bock's Car* (5–1). This plane carried three additional officers: navy captain Frederick L. Ashworth as weaponeer (5–2), his assistant, Second Lieutenant Philip M. Barnes (5–3), and First Lieutenant Jacob Beser, who had the highly specialized task of ensuring that the Japanese did not jam the frequencies upon which the bomb's fuse operated. Ash-

5-1: Crew Members of Nagasaki Mission— August 9, 1945

Bock's Car

Maj. Charles W. Sweeney	Squadron Commander and Pilot
Capt. Frederick L. Ashworth, USN	Weaponeer
1st Lt. Charles D. Albury	Copilot
Capt. James F. Van Pelt, Jr.	Navigator
Capt. Kermit K. Beahan	Bombardier
1st Lt. Jacob Beser	Radar Countermeasures
2nd Lt. Fred J. Olivi	Asst. Copilot
2nd Lt. Philip M. Barnes*	Asst. Weaponeer
M/Sgt. John D. Kuharek	Flight Engineer
S/Sgt. Edward R. Buckley	Radar Operator
Sgt. Abe M. Spitzer	Radio Operator
Sgt. Albert T. DeHart	Tail Gunner
Sgt. Raymond G. Gallagher	Aviation Mechanic/ Gunner

The Great Artiste—Victor 89

Capt. Frederick C. Bock, Jr.	Pilot
2nd Lt. Hugh C. Ferguson	Copilot
2nd Lt. Leonard A. Godrey	Navigator
1st Lt. Charles Levy	Bombardier
M/Sgt. Roderick F. Arnold	Flight Engineer
S/Sgt. Ralph D. Curry	Radio Operator
S/Sgt. William C. Barney	Radar Operator
S/Sgt. Robert J. Stock	Tail Gunner
Sgt. Ralph D. Belanger	Scanner

*Lieutenant Barnes was borrowed from the 1st Ordnance Squadron.

5-2 Captain Frederick L. Ashworth, USN, as a commander circa 1943. He served as weaponeer for the Nagasaki bomb.

5-3 Second Lieutenant Phillip M. Barnes, Ashworth's assistant weaponeer.

5-4 Fat Man, the Nagasaki bomb, toggled out of *Bock's Car* by Captain Kermit K. Beahan at 10:58 A.M. Nagasaki time on August 9, 1945.

worth had already played a key role in the atomic bomb story. In February 1945, he had delivered a letter to Admiral Nimitz informing him of the development of the atomic bomb. And it was he who had selected the northwest corner of Tinian as a base for the 509th. Beser was the only man who flew to both Hiroshima and Nagasaki in the aircraft that actually dropped the bombs. The third aircraft on the Nagasaki mission, captained by Major James T. Hopkins, carried the movie cameras and some British scientific observers.

During the preflight briefing, Tibbets told them that the second bomb would make the Hiroshima bomb obsolete. Called Fat Man because of its rotund shape, this bomb had a core of plutonium-239 surrounded by gunpowder (5–4). The result was an internal implosive rather than explosive force. The bomb measured 128 inches in length, with a diameter of 60 inches, and it weighed almost $4\frac{1}{4}$ tons.

At the briefing, weather experts announced that because a typhoon was threatening over Iwo Jima, the ren-

5–5 Crew of squadron commander Sweeney. Standing (l–r): Captain Kermit K. Beahan; Captain James F. Van Pelt, Jr.; First Lieutenant Charles D. Albury; Second Lieutenant Fred J. Olivi; Major Charles W. Sweeney. Kneeling (l–r): Staff Sergeant Edward R. Buckley; Master Sergeant John D. Kuharek; Sergeant Raymond G. Gallagher; Staff Sergeant Albert D. DeHart; Sergeant Abe M. Spitzer. Not pictured are First Lieutenant Jacob Beser, radar countermeasures; Captain Frederick L. Ashworth, USN, weaponeer; Second Lieutenant Philip M. Barnes, assistant weaponeer.

dezvous point would be Yakushima, off the Kyushu coast. Four B-29s had been deployed as rescue planes in case of a ditching. The crew was cautioned that the bomb drop must be made visually lest the result be unfruitful. After a prayer by Chaplain Downey and a light meal, the men were ready to emplane.

As they had for *Enola Gay,* klieg lights lit up the scene; cameramen and brass abounded, while Sweeney's crew posed for a group photo (5–5). As they had during *Enola Gay*'s preparations for takeoff, men from the 509th clustered around to wish Sweeney and his men well (5–6). Perhaps envious, perhaps thankful—either emotion would have been understandable—First Lieutenant Ralph N. Devore, one of the 393rd's aircraft commanders, chatted briefly with Sweeney (5–7). Sweeney was a busy man, making last-minute checks of the navigation charts (5–8) and of *Bock's Car* (5–9)—not, after all, his own *Great Artiste,* which he knew inch for inch. Before takeoff, Staff Sergeant Ralph D. Curry, Bock's radio operator in *The Great Artiste,* asked a scientist standing nearby: "What's this bomb going to do?" The

expert replied, "I don't know, son—it may blow you out of the sky!"—hardly a reassuring reply.

Indeed, *Bock's Car* and its escorts had no such comparatively smooth operation as *Enola Gay* had experienced. Shortly before takeoff, the flight engineer, Master Sergeant John D. Kuharek, found that one of the fuel pumps was not operating, trapping 600 gallons of gas. This loss, which could easily mean the difference between a safe return and disaster, offered ample reason to cancel an ordinary mission. But it was considered essential to drop the second bomb as soon as possible, to convince the Japanese that Hiroshima had not been an isolated event and that the United States could deliver the "rain of ruin" of which Truman had spoken. So, after a brief discussion, Sweeney decided to go forward.

Takeoff, at 1:56 A.M., was a cliff-hanger. The weight of the Fat Man pinned the B-29 to the runway until the last possible second. Then, a little over an hour later, Dr. Robert Serber, the high-speed-camera specialist, who was supposed to be in Hopkins's photographic plane, walked into headquarters. Hopkins had scratched him

5-6 Irwin talks with copilot Albury, while behind Irwin, radio operator Spitzer passes the moment with cigar-toting Sweeney.

5-7 First Lieutenant Ralph N. Devore, one of the airplane commanders from the 393rd Bombardment Squadron, talks with Sweeney before takeoff.

5-8 One last check on the navigation charts by Van Pelt, Sweeney, and Olivi.

5-9 Armed with flashlight and cigar, Sweeney checks out *Bock's Car* before takeoff in the early-morning hours of August 9.

because he had forgotten his parachute. Only Serber knew how to operate the specialized equipment, so headquarters had no choice but to break radio silence and brief Hopkins on the camera's mysteries.

All the aircraft on the mission encountered bad weather; however, both weather planes reported favorable conditions over the targets. But for a heart-stopping half hour, matters were far from favorable in *Bock's Car.* Ashworth and Barnes were horrified to note the red arming light had come on in the black box connected to the Fat Man, indicating that the firing circuit had closed. Working with cool efficiency, Barnes found that a failed switch had caused a malfunction. He corrected the problem and all was well once more.

Bock's Car and *The Great Artiste* rendezvoused at Yakushima. Bock, piloting *The Great Artiste,* had caught a glimpse of Hopkins's observation plane, but Sweeney never saw it, and after circling for some forty minutes had to give up. He signaled Bock, and the two planes headed for Kokura.

A city of about 110,000, Kokura was of real interest to the bombing mission only as the site of a huge arsenal serving the Japanese army. Sweeney's men were under orders to bomb visually, and only the precise target would do. But haze and smoke obscured the arsenal and three runs were unsuccessful. In addition, the anti-aircraft guns of this heavily defended city were coming dangerously close to the range, and fighter aircraft were rising. These facts, plus the ever-lower fuel supply, dictated second thoughts. So Sweeney, Ashworth, and bombardier Captain Kermit K. Beahan decided to head for the second target. And this time, if visual sighting proved impossible, they would resort to radar. This was contrary to orders, but Ashworth took the responsibility because of the fuel shortage. So Kokura proceeded about its daily business, unaware how narrowly it had escaped Nagasaki's fate.

In the 1940s, Nagasaki had a population of roughly 212,000. The city had a mild climate and a charming locale on the west coast of Kyushu at the head of Nagasaki Bay. The city is open in that direction, but hills protect its other three sides (5–10). This hilly, almost mountain-

5-10 An annotated aerial view of Nagasaki. This is a reconnaissance mosaic.

1. TATEGAMI SHIPYARD
2. MITSUBISHI DOCKYARD
3. AKUNOURA ENGINE WORKS
4. MITSUBISHI ELECTRIC MFG. CO
5. NAGASAKI & DEJIMA WHARVES &
    R. R. YARDS
6. MITSUBISHI STEEL & ARMS WORKS
7. MITSUBISHI-URAKAMI ORDNANCE PLANT

STATUTE MILE

5-11 Customs House for the port of Nagasaki.

5-12 Nagasaki Prefecture Courthouse.

ous terrain would make Nagasaki a much different and more difficult target than Hiroshima.

In the sixteenth century, Nagasaki's harbor teemed with ships from Portugal, Spain, and Holland, while Japanese ships left port for other trading centers in Asia. With the period of isolation beginning in 1637, only the Dutch (confined to the small island of Deshima in the bay*) and the Chinese were permitted. Throughout those centuries, some of Nagasaki's people clung in secret to the Catholic faith they had adopted at the time of St. Francis Xavier. With the Meiji Restoration these Christians emerged; by 1914, Our Lady of the Immaculate Conception, the largest Catholic cathedral in Japan, had risen in the Urakami district. It was, however, of less historic interest than the Catholic church at Oura, which dated from 1864 and ranked as a national treasure.

In general, however, Nagasaki seemed more oriented to the present than to the past. Modern Japanese architects were quite enamored of the Western art deco building style, with its flowing, streamlined curves. In areas where modern buildings such as the Customs House (5–11) predominated, this motif was quite common and was very much in step with the Japanese desire to compete with the West. The prefecture courthouse (5–12) was typical of the low-profile, understated government buildings found in Japanese cities. The cultural mind-set fostered an affinity for the small, although perhaps elegantly decorated—an attitude that extended into the prevailing architecture.

*Deshima has been reclaimed as part of the mainland.

5-13 Ohato Street, Nagasaki. Note the electric streetcar.

Like many other Japanese cities, Nagasaki had a very high proportion of wooden structures, few of which rose higher than two stories (5–13). Residential streets (5–14) leading up into the terraced hills out from the river were narrow, winding, and so steep that steps had to be cut into them. This hilly topography made use of hand-drawn fire equipment particularly difficult. Still, modern fire vehicles were something of a rarity in Japan outside the larger cities (5–15).

A view of Nagasaki's downtown shopping area (5–16) is typical. Oddly enough, the picture of Nagasaki's main police station (5–17), like many other photos from the Strategic Bombing Survey, comes from a prewar post-card. These were an important source of data concerning many Axis cities, both in Japan and Germany. A Nagasaki landmark that survived the bombing was the rail-road station (5–18). As it had for centuries, much activity centered on water traffic, small as well as large (5–19).

5-14 Typical residential quarter in Nagasaki.

5-15 This particular firehouse in Nagasaki proudly displays "No. 3," a modern pumper unit.

5-16 One of Nagasaki's downtown shopping areas.

5-17 Nagasaki's main police station (right) in the city's mercantile district.

5-18 Nagasaki Railroad Station.

5-19 Small boats lie nestled together in a tributary of the Nakeshima River.

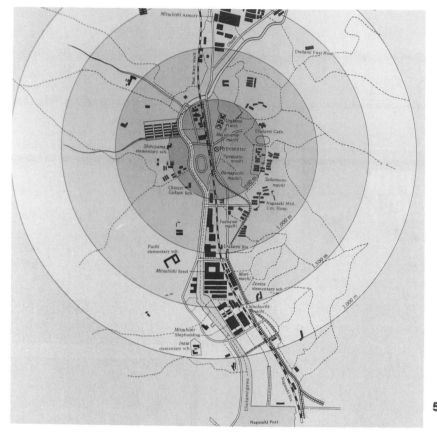

5–20 Nagasaki, 10:58 A.M., August 9, 1945.

Many Western music lovers had a soft spot for Nagasaki as the setting of Puccini's wistful *Madama Butterfly.* Of more practical interest to the U.S. military was the fact that two of Mitsubishi's great war plants were located in Nagasaki. This was the target. Nothing else would be good enough. Had sheer terrorism been the aim, any location over the city would have sufficed, but the principal object was to deal a telling blow to Japan's war effort. And *Bock's Car* carried only one bomb.

The weather over Nagasaki was not much of an improvement over Kokura's, and 90 percent of the run was by radar. At the last possible moment, Beahan spotted a break in the cloud cover and made the drop at 10:58 A.M. Nagasaki time (5–20). If Beahan had had perfect visibil-

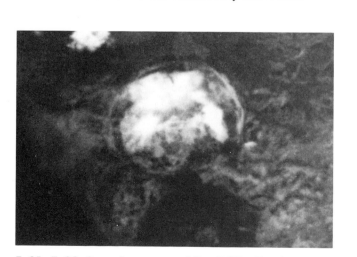

5–21, 5–22 Seen from one of the B-29s, the fireball boils upward from Nagasaki one minute after Beahan dropped the bomb.

ity and all the time in the world, he could not have done much better. The Fat Man exploded over a spot approximately 500 feet to the south of the Mitsubishi Steel and Armament Works. Within a minute, a brilliant fireball erupted upward (5–21 and 5–22). Sweeney banked sharply to avoid the danger. The atomic cloud over Nagasaki was at least as awesome as that over Hiroshima. It sprang upward, constantly changing shape and color (5–23 and 5–24). As Sergeant Albert T. (Pappy) DeHart, *Bock's Car's* tail gunner, excitedly filmed the scene, five successive shock waves battered the B-29s. The radioactive cloud moved nearer, and Sweeney turned away. *Bock's Car* and *The Great Artiste* headed homeward.

5–23, 5–24 From two different vantage points, the mushroom cloud continues its climb toward the stratosphere.

The successful release from the strain they had been under gave the men's spirits a boost, but bad luck had not stopped toying with the mission. The approximately 300 gallons of gas remaining would not take them to Tinian, and even Okinawa would be a tight squeeze. So Sweeney had radio operator Sergeant Abe Spitzer try to contact the air-sea rescue mission to alert them to the possibility of a ditching. He received no answer; the rescue people had shut down, evidently assuming that the B-29s had long since returned to Tinian.

The arrival at Okinawa was equally bizarre. Repeated attempts to raise a tower—any tower—brought no response. Other aircraft were taking off and landing, and *Bock's Car* did not have enough gas for protracted circling. In desperation Sweeney ordered flares set off, and finally somebody noticed. The landing, at two P.M. local

time, was rough but successful. Kuharek drained and measured the remaining gas. It came to seven gallons. The emergency happily over, *Bock's Car* refueled, took off, and by 11:39 P.M. had reached Tinian safely.

Homecoming was definitely an anticlimax. The Hiroshima fliers had received a hero's welcome, but no one was on hand to greet the Nagasaki group. Apparently the second atomic mission had already become routine. Worse yet, no one had thought to have food ready for these famished men, who had not eaten for about twenty-two hours. A mess attendant made a lame, belated offer of pancakes. "Some big deal!" snorted Staff Sergeant Curry from *The Great Artiste*.

The indifference accorded Sweeney and his men, oddly enough, presaged public perception of Nagasaki, or lack of it. As the events of World War II became less

5-25

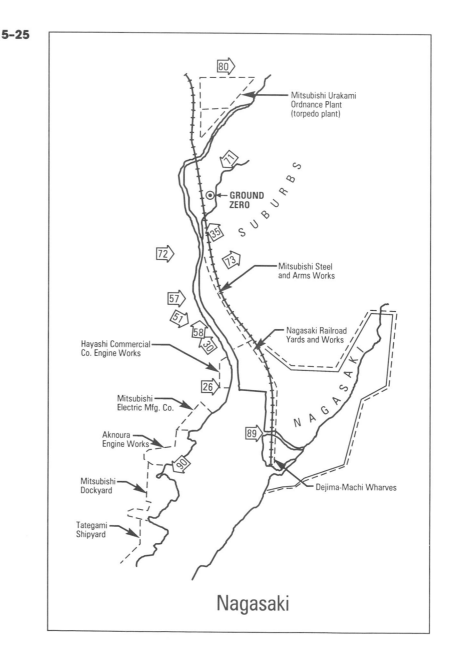

Nagasaki

living memories than history, the word "Hiroshima" still rang a bell; a mention of Nagasaki frequently drew a blank stare. Yet Nagasaki, too, is worth remembering.

The city did not experience a firestorm such as had wrought so much devastation at Hiroshima. Apparently, however, the blast was more destructive, because of the bowl-shaped topography and the power of the second bomb. (Vantage points of the aerial photographs may be seen in 5–25.) The explosion swept down the river val-ley, leaving behind a swath of destruction in the areas close to the river, while having comparatively little effect on sectors that enjoyed the protection of an intervening hillside (5–26).

According to *The United States Army Air Forces in World War II,* in an area roughly 2.3 miles by 1.9 miles, all buildings were either destroyed outright or damaged beyond use (5–27 and 5–28). Beyond this core lay an area of severe damage that included the Urakami section

5–26 This view of the port facility of Nagasaki, 7,500 feet from the hypocenter, provides a graphic illustration of the "acoustics" of the bomb blast.

5–27 Annotated aerial mosaic of Nagasaki several days after the bombing.

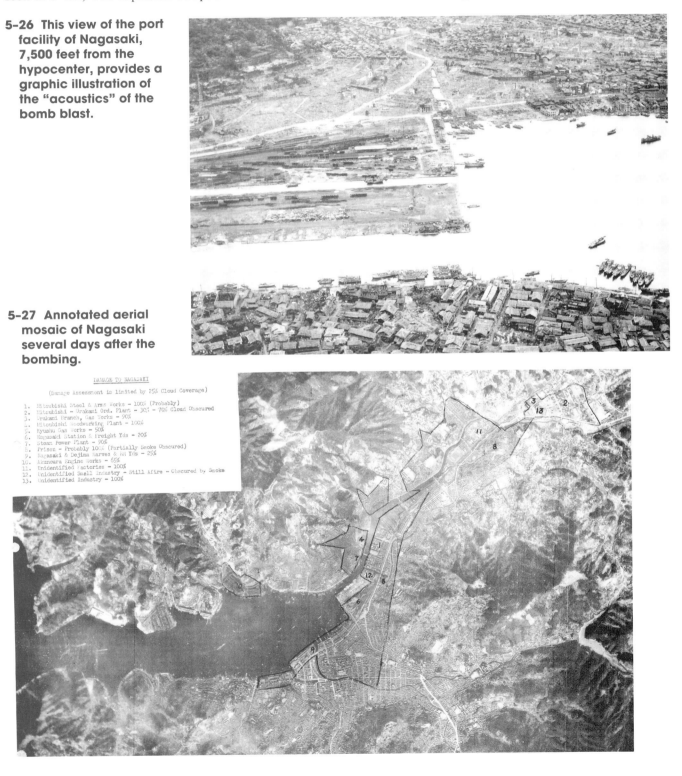

DAMAGE TO NAGASAKI

(Damage Assessment is limited by 25% Cloud Coverage)

1. Mitsubishi Steel & Arms Works - 100% (Probably)
2. Mitsubishi - Urakami Ord. Plant - 30% - 70% Cloud Obscured
3. Urakami Branch, Gas Works - 90%
4. Mitsubishi Woodworking Plant - 100%
5. Kyushu Gas Works - 50%
6. Nagasaki Station & Freight Yds - 20%
7. Steam Power Plant - 90%
8. Prison - Probably 100% (Partially Smoke Obscured)
9. Nagasaki & Dejima Warves & RR Yds - 25%
10. Akunoura Engine Works - 65%
11. Unidentified Factories - 100%
12. Unidentified Small Industry - Still Afire - Obscured by Smoke
13. Unidentified Industry - 100%

5-28 Aerial photo of the city showing ground zero and concentric circles half a mile and one mile out from the hypocenter.

5-29 The featureless plain of the Urakami River valley within half a mile of ground zero.

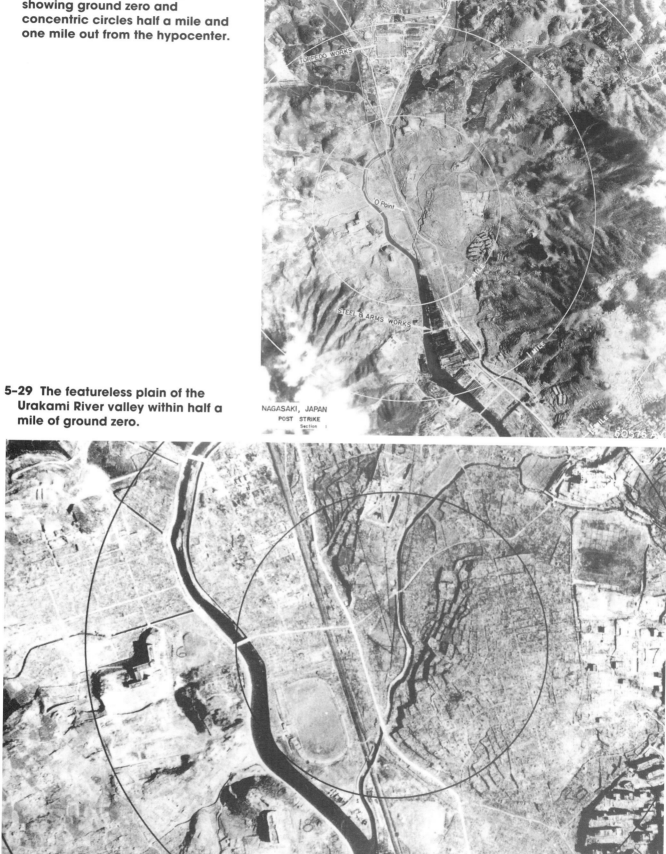

**5-30 At 5,000 feet from the hypocenter, a residential area on the west bank of the
Urakami borders a logging operation slightly downriver from the Mitsubishi complex.**

and both sides of the harbor (5–29). Yet the total area of destruction was later established as 1.45 square miles of the city's 3.86, which was less than at Hiroshima and just a little more than half the results from conventional incendiary raids. Photo 5–30 shows a residential area about 500 feet from ground zero on the west bank of the Urakami River, bordering a logging operation. Although the dwellings sustained some damage, they were not flattened as at the same distance at Hiroshima.

As with the latter, the exact number of casualties was impossible to assess. The Japanese cited only verifiable cases, so their official estimate of 23,753 killed, 1,927 missing, and 23,345 wounded is undoubtedly too conservative. Later U.S. Strategic Bombing Survey figures were much higher, but still below those for Hiroshima.

Nevertheless, Nagasaki's citizens were in no position to make objective comparisons between their experience and Hiroshima's. To them it was all horrible, as doubtless it was to the Japanese soldiers in photo 5–31. Composite photos 5–32 and 5–33 give some idea of what met the eyes of survivors.

5-31 Japanese soldiers rummage through the ruins of the city.

5-32 A panorama of four photos taken from ground zero, west at center. The two large schools near the hypocenter, Chinzei and Shiroyama, lie at the left and center, respectively.

5-33 A panorama of four photos taken from ground zero, northeast at center. At left center is the Urakami River valley. Just out of the panorama at right is the Nagasaki Medical College.

5–34 Nagasaki from near ground zero.

No wonder the Nagasaki Prefecture Report characterized the area as "like a graveyard without a tombstone standing" (5–34).

Photo 5–35 portrays a portion of the city near ground zero looking northwest. While photo 5–36 shows an area 1,000 feet from ground zero to the northeast. At the $\frac{1}{4}$-mile distance, a reinforced concrete stack had been snapped off (5–37). A school at roughly the same distance was gutted (5–38). At 1,500 feet, a streetcar was blown six feet off the track (5–39).

5–35 The vicinity of ground zero on the Urakami River looking northwest. The athletic complex here served Chinzei School (just out of the picture at left) and Shiroyama Elementary School at upper left.

5–36 Northeast of ground zero, 1,000 feet out.

5–37 A reinforced-concrete chimney stack snapped off by the explosion lies $1/4$ mile from the center of the blast.

5–38 Beam, ceiling, and column failure as seen in a school's interior $1/4$ mile from the explosion.

5–39 At 1,500 feet from the hypocenter a streetcar sits, blown six feet off the track.

5–40 At 2,500 feet out, steel-and-concrete buildings stand, but little else does. The roof of the small church at center (note the adjacent cemetery) has collapsed, along with one of the gables.

5–41 An entire row of small trees lies flat, snapped off close to the ground at 2,700 feet.

At the 2,500-foot radius, buildings constructed of steel and concrete remained standing, but little else survived (5–40). Two hundred feet farther out, a row of trees was snapped off near the ground (5–41). The intense heat at ground zero blistered roofing tiles (5–42), and bridges sustained damage similar to that suffered at Hiroshima (5–43). Some reinforced concrete walls near the hypocenter look as if they had been ruffled in a high wind (5–44). As at Hiroshima, some underground air-raid shelters survived (5–45).

5–42 A roofing tile blistered by intense heat at ground zero.

5-43 This bridge sustained damage reminiscent of the sort suffered at Hiroshima. Note the concrete guardrails resting in the streambed at some distance from the bridge.

5-44 Reinforced concrete walls of certain buildings near ground zero exhibited an uncanny windblown appearance.

5-45 Underground bomb shelters dug into an earthen mound near ground zero.

Although, as has been mentioned, there was no firestorm at Nagasaki, fires did break out in the central city and river valley, destroying entire residential areas (5–46). Nearly two miles out, the blast itself, as well as fire, destroyed locations in its path (5–47).

At 8,200 to 8,800 feet, damage was still considerable (5–48 and 5–49). Beyond that, it tapered off. Just over 1½ miles from the detonation, wooden residences still stood erect with relatively minor damage; this was particularly true of those protected by intervening hills. Much of the threat to these homes came from the fires spreading quickly from the city center. The firebreak at left saved this particular neighborhood (5–50).

5–46 Fire destroyed entire residential areas of the city, including some sheltered areas. Here, a firebreak saved the houses on the hillside from suffering the same fate as those on the other side of the firebreak.

5–47 At 9,600 feet, areas directly in the path of the blast coming down the river valley were destroyed, by both fire and blast damage.

5-48 Nagasaki's old police station sits amid devastation, 8,200 feet from ground zero. Note the intact housing at right.

5-49 All wooden buildings in the vicinity of Nakamachi Church were destroyed, 8,800 feet from the center.

5-50 Wooden houses still stand at approximately 1$\frac{1}{2}$ miles from ground zero.

5-51 View looking southeast toward the mouth of the Urakami, where the river widens to an estuary at Nagasaki's port facility at far right.

Later it was estimated that Nagasaki's industry suffered a 68.3 percent loss—more severe than Hiroshima's. Industries and shipyard facilities lined the Urakami River south of photo 5–51. An ordnance factory 750 feet from ground zero was wrecked (5–52). Even past the mile mark, evidence abounded of industrial damage. A storage tank at the Yachiyo-Machi Gas Works collapsed (5–53), while the downward pressure caved in the tops of those tanks not collapsed (5–54). At a container-manufacturing facility, a row of gas bottles revealed the direction of the blast (5–55).

5-52 Wreckage of an ordnance factory 750 feet from ground zero. The stacks standing at the center are visible at right in 5-32.

5-53 This storage tank at the Yachiyo-Machi Gas Works collapses under the force of the blast at 6,600 feet from ground zero.

5-54 Even from more than a mile distant, the terrific downward pressure wave caved in the tops of tanks not collapsed.

5-55 A collapsed row of gas bottles shoved to the right at this container-manufacturing facility testifies to the direction of the blast.

5–56 **The sprawling Mitsubishi Steel and Armament Works, $^3/_5$ mile downriver from ground zero.**

Of particular interest to the Americans was the wiping out of the prime target, the Mitsubishi Steel and Armament Works (5–56, 5–57, and 5–58). This complex stretched south from a point 2,000 feet from the hypocenter, extending along the east bank of the Urakami River for nearly half a mile. The wrecked machine shop shown in 5–59 was at approximately the 4,000-foot mark. Like virtually all of the facilities, Mitsubishi's torpedo-assembly plant, $^2/_3$ mile north of ground zero, was thoroughly wrecked (5–60). Photo 5–61 shows

5–57 **The Mitsubishi Works along the eastern shore of the Urakami River, $^2/_3$ mile south.**

5-58 The great Mitsubishi complex, looking north up the Urakami River.

5-59 This wrecked machine shop of the Mitsubishi complex lay at approximately the 4,000-foot mark. Note the machines torn from their foundations by collapsing steel members from the ceiling.

5-60 Note how the upright girders have been pushed over at about 10 degrees at the Mitsubishi torpedo-assembly plant.

5-61 Torpedo-assembly equipment.

5-62 Collapsed ceilings and walls in the torpedo plant.

torpedo-assembly equipment, while 5–62 reveals a collapsed ceiling and walls in the plant. Being impossible to bulldoze, this wreckage would take months to blow up, cut away, and clear.

Downriver 5,000 feet away, an electrical switchboard had been upended and partially burnt (5–63). At about the same distance out, an occasional sturdy wooden structure in a protected area still stood, although with heavy blast damage and some fire damage (5–64). At 11,120 feet south of ground zero, buildings suffered only minor blast damage. The grader at right in photo 5–65 probably constructed the firebreak in the foreground. Moving 12,000 feet southeast of the epicenter, roofing tiles and fascia boards experienced superficial damage (5–66), while another 1,000 feet farther southeast, some

5-63 Downriver, 5,000 feet south from the hypocenter, this electrical switchboard lies upended and damaged by fire.

5-64 At 5,000 feet out from the center, an occasional wooden structure survived, although damaged by blast and fire.

5-65 Structures 11,120 feet south of ground zero exhibit only blast damage. In the foreground is a firebreak, likely constructed with the aid of the grader at right.

5-66 At 12,000 feet southeast there is superficial damage, including roofing tiles and fascia board knocked away.

5–67 At 13,000 feet southeast: an occasional light wall blown over.

light walls had fallen (5–67). Still another 1,000 feet, and the foreign-style house in photo 5–68 escaped with only loosened roofing tiles. At last, at 14,125 feet—nearly 2⅔ miles—from ground zero, buildings were undamaged (5–69).

One of the more deplorable aspects of the atomic bomb is the fact that it cannot be used selectively. No matter how carefully the planners may choose, and the bombardier pinpoint, the target, many nonmilitary and cultural centers, and thousands of people, will also be obliterated.

That morning, hundreds of people filled the Cathedral of Our Lady of the Immaculate Conception (5–70), waiting to make their confessions in anticipation of the Feast Day of the Assumption. The atomic blast brought down the roof and other parts of the cathedral, killing every worshiper. A similar fate but in a very different setting befell the guards and prisoners at the Nagasaki Branch Prison. Only sections of the walls aligned in the direction of the blast survived (5–71).

5–68 At 14,000 feet southeast: loosened roofing on this well-built foreign-style house.

5-69 At 14,125 feet southwest of ground zero: at last, undamaged dwellings, nearly 2²/₃ miles from the hypocenter.

5-70 Urakami Cathedral, one of Nagasaki's prominent landmarks, stands on a hill amid the rubble of a residential district east of ground zero.

5-71 View looking southwest toward ground zero and the Urakami River from a point ¹/₄ mile distant. Note the terraced ground at left in one of the city's residential areas. In the foreground are the ruins of Urakami Prison.

5-72 Looking east across the Urakami River valley toward the ruins of Nagasaki Medical College nestled against the hills beyond. Ground zero is almost out of the photo at left.

One of Japan's best hospitals, that of Nagasaki University, was destroyed (5–72), as was the Nagasaki Medical College. The twin red-and-white smokestacks of the facility, shown in the center of photos 5–73 and 5–74, were prominent landmarks, and later aided in orienting much postwar photography of the area. The explosion 2,000 feet distant crooked one of the stacks. The loss of the medical facilities seriously hampered treatment of the thousands of burned and lacerated victims. An esti-

mated half of Nagasaki's medical personnel were killed, and many of those living were too shocked to do anything but run for shelter.

A postwar photographer seemed particularly intrigued with the Nagasaki Medical College and took a series of pictures. Turning left after shooting photo 5–74, he moved halfway down the hill, and snapped photo 5–75. At the bottom of the hill, he walked between the two far buildings to photograph still further damage (5–76).

5-73 Closer view of the Nagasaki Medical College complex, 2,500 feet from ground zero.

5-74 Another scene of ruin, 500 yards south of the cathedral, this time at Nagasaki Medical College. Shiroyama School lies across the valley.

5-75 The photographer turns left, walks out of the previous picture at right, moves down among the buildings halfway down the hill, turns, and takes another photo.

5-76 Ending his trek down the hill, the photographer walks between the two far buildings at center in 5-75 to record yet more devastation.

5-77 Nothing remains of the college's wooden storehouse here, except for ashes and a low mound of melted glass.

Although the college buildings seemed intact, the intense heat from the explosion and the fires that followed destroyed most of their contents (5–77). Interior spaces of the college's concrete building fared little better. In photo 5–78, debris from upper floors has smashed into an operating room. The entire contents of an examination and record-storage room were reduced to a one-foot layer of fine gray ash (5–79).

Schools and athletic facilities such as that shown in photo 5–80 also suffered devastation. This establishment had the misfortune to be located close to the Mitsubishi complex, as did the Shiroyama School (5–81).

5-78 Here, debris crashed into an operating room from several floors above.

5-79 Fire completely destroyed the contents of this examination and record-storage room.

5-80 An athletic complex in the vicinity of the Mitsubishi Armory, one mile north of ground zero.

5-81 On September 29, 1945, an unnamed Signal Corps photographer strolled out to the arch, faced northwest, and took this picture of the Mitsubishi factory at left and Shiroyama School in the background against the hills at right.

From the cathedral steps a photographer snapped this view of the Chinzei School (5–82), which also appears in photo 5–83, looking from the Urakami River's east bank. From a distance, the structure seemed intact, but an aerial view reveals that the entire roof had caved in (5–84). It is evident, however, from the mass of machine tools found on Chinzei's first floor, that the institution was not entirely devoted to academics. Obviously munitions work had been carried out (5–85).

Residences, of course, were much less able to withstand the blast than the sturdier public buildings. Photo 5–86 shows one residential area, about 1,000 feet from ground zero. A mile farther out, plaster-and-bamboo

5-82 A sad spectacle indeed greeted the photographer who, from the cathedral steps, peered across the Urakami River valley and through the mist toward ruined Chinzei School.

5-83 Chinzei School from the east bank of the Urakami River.

5-84 A view from the air shows that, although from a distance Chinzei School appears to be intact, the entire roof has fallen in onto the building's third floor.

5-85 Before the bombing, munitions work proceeded apace, as evidenced by the machine tools seen here on Cinzei's first floor.

5-86 A residential area just east of ground zero, 1,000 feet out from the hypocenter. Urakami Cathedral lies in the distance.

5–87 Residential structures at the mile mark, with their plaster-and-bamboo-lath exterior walls, were still no match for Fat Man's power.

walls could not withstand the blast (5–87). Some displaced persons erected emergency shelters from the debris near the cathedral (5–88). Behind the waterfront, about two miles from ground zero (5–89), fires consumed many buildings. The surviving structures this far out likely were saved by firebreaks and the tributary at right, which flowed into the Urakami. At 2¼ miles from ground zero, structures along the estuary sustained the greatest damage, while residential areas away from the shipyards and dry docks remained intact (5–90).

Bewildered and stunned citizens able to do so walked toward who knows what destination (5–91). A sign near the Nagasaki Medical College indicated the place name of the Urakami Railroad Station (5–92). At that depot

5–88 In the shadows of the cathedral, Nagasaki citizens bereft of regular housing have erected impromptu hovels from the debris around them. Note the tarpaulin on the "house" at right.

5-89 Farther down the estuary from 5-26, approximately two miles from ground zero, fires consumed a large area behind the waterfront.

5-90 At $2^1/_4$ miles from the hypocenter, on the west bank of the estuary, residential areas away from the shipyard and dry-dock area remain intact. Structures along the estuary received the lion's share of the bomb's wrath.

5-91 Nagasaki's bewildered and stunned citizens trudge down a city street in the wake of the atomic explosion. This is a Japanese photograph.

5-92 Facing northeast, a photographer looked across the platform toward Nagasaki Medical College at far right. Just under the college buildings is a signboard bearing the two kanji characters for the station's place name, Ura-kami. Also note the Shinto arch, left of the sign, which aroused the curiosity of at least one other photographer.

passengers hopefully waited for a train (5- 93). Farther south, at Nagasaki Station, service continued uninterrupted. As at Hiroshima, a dirty black rain fell on Urakami, adding a final dismal note to the suffering of the already frightened and distressed people. But at least the rain served to put out some of the fires. All told, so little of its infrastructure remained functional that Nagasaki's road to recovery would be long and arduous.

5-93 Passengers line up, waiting for the train at Urakami station, which lay to the rear of the gutted Mitsubishi armaments factory, looking west from the platform.

CHAPTER 6

Peace!

The Japanese government had entertained a faint hope that the Soviet Union, technically neutral in the Pacific war, would act as intermediary with the Allies in arranging a negotiated peace. But Moscow had kept Ambassador Naotake Sato dangling for weeks. At last, on August 8, Foreign Minister Vyacheslav Molotov had agreed to meet with Sato, who hoped to arrange for former premier Prince Fumimaro Konoye (6–1) to travel to Moscow as Japan's representative.

Instead, one day later, the Soviet Union declared war on Japan. Now, also on August 9, the second atomic bomb had been dropped, yet the Supreme War Direction Council remained deadlocked. When Togo first proposed acceptance of the Potsdam Declaration, "no one would venture an opinion," Toyoda recalled, "and an ominous silence reigned in the conference room."

Finally, Navy Minister Admiral Mitsumasa Yonai (6–2) suggested that they take up such questions as

6-1 Prince Fumimaro Konoye (left) and Vice Admiral Mitsumasa Yonai (right), navy minister in Suzuki's cabinet.

6-2 Vice Admiral Mitsumasa Yonai, Suzuki's navy minister.

whether acceptance should be unconditional, and if they attached conditions, what those should be. Should they study such questions as the Emperor system, disarmament, war criminals, and the occupation of Japan? Obviously Yonai was merely trying to get the discussion moving, because when Togo promptly declared that Japan should propose nothing beyond the preservation of the Emperor system, Yonai readily agreed.

With this the lines were evenly drawn. Prime Minister Admiral Baron Kantaro Suzuki, Togo, and Yonai favored immediate acceptance with that one proviso; Minister of War General Korechika Anami, Chief of the Army General Staff General Yoshijiro Umezu, and Toyoda insisted upon three additional conditions: There would be no occupation, or a very limited one, of Japan's main islands; the Japanese should conduct their own disarmament; and the Japanese should try their own war criminals. These three officers were not fools, and must have known how absurd were these provisos under the circumstances. Certainly the Japanese never granted any such leniency in the areas they conquered. Togo pointed out that presentation of these conditions would almost certainly bring an Allied refusal to negotiate further. This, obviously, was what the three holdouts wanted, so Togo's protest did not sway them. Anami remarked in effect that Japan had not yet lost the war, and if the enemy tried to land on the Home Islands he would regret it. Umezu added that the Japanese might be able to push the invaders into the sea, and that even if they did land, their losses would be prohibitive.

They referred to Operation Ketsu Go No. 6, the defense of Kyushu, which the Japanese had been preparing for months in anticipation of an American invasion. And those preparations had been formidable. In the words of General Shigeru Hasunuma, aide-de-camp to the Emperor, "all available first-class troops had been withdrawn from China and Manchuria for the crucial battle on the Japanese mainland." As a result, more than a million armed and equipped fighting men were in the Home Islands. Inventory as of June 30 showed enough ammunition for twelve divisions, a month's supply of food for 2,100,000 men, and a month's medical supplies for 11,600,000 cases. By the end of July, 90 percent of the planned units had arrived from Korea and Manchuria, and munitions had been stored in Kyushu—50 percent in caves and 50 percent in "schools, homes, etc."

Not much help could be expected from the once-mighty naval and air forces. One naval officer expressed doubt that the navy could even defend the Inland Sea. A survey as of July 1 showed that the navy had 5,045 aircraft on hand, of which 3,566 were operational. And of these, more than one half were training aircraft. So airpower's principal contribution would have to be kamikazes.

Nevertheless, many officers were cautiously optimistic, especially as to an initial landing attempt. It was estimated that the Japanese could destroy about half of the U.S. forces offshore "by Army and Navy special* attacks, small craft special attacks, and division coastal batteries." The object was to inflict damage to the Americans sufficient to cause the United States to have second thoughts and, as Lieutenant General Torashiro Kawabe, assistant chief of the general staff, explained, "Thus the war would be brought to an end that would be comparatively favorable for us." From first to last, the Japanese military underestimated American tenacity.

Realists, however, understood that whatever success might crown the initial encounter, Japan lacked sufficient power to handle successive assaults. So now Togo countered Anami and Umezu by remarking that their assurances might be true of the first assault, but what would happen after that? Having sacrificed its remaining munitions, Japan would be truly helpless.

Umezu came forth with the real reason for the intransigence: For Japanese fighting men, surrender was not possible. In fact, it was a military crime. He doubted that the men at the various fronts would obey such an order. Umezu was not being bombastic; he was expressing a fact of Japanese military life so fundamental that he and his colleagues, no less than their juniors, were fast in its grip. One died fighting, if necessary; surrender was quite simply unthinkable.

Yonai, no less than Anami, Umezu, and Toyoda, had been trained in this tradition, and it took a very particular type of courage to swim against the tide. But Yonai had a large streak of common sense. He had opposed a military alliance with Germany so outspokenly that the army had brought down his brief prewar premiership, and made him no stranger to threats of assassination. Now he pointed out that, while the proposed conditions undoubtedly would be favorable for Japan, it was too late for such bargaining.

Anami had a weapon at his disposal that could have brought the whole process to a screeching halt. If he had resigned as minister of war, and if the army refused to appoint a replacement, the Suzuki cabinet would have fallen, and no new one could have been formed. This was the hammerlock the military held on civilian Japan: According to the constitution, the ministers of war and the navy had to be flag officers on active duty. To his credit, Anami did not resort to this action.

The meeting remained deadlocked, and Suzuki adjourned it, having shrewdly avoided a formal vote. But the old sailor, at seventy-eight a hero of the Russo-Japanese War, still had a long day's work ahead of him. At 2:30 that afternoon he convened the full cabinet.

---

* i. e., suicide.

Umezu and Toyoda were not members, so they were absent, but Anami was there, in full voice, his views unshaken. Consequently the cabinet session was, as Togo put it, "a repeat performance" of the earlier meeting, with this major difference: The civil ministries had their say. Their news was not good—the rice crop was the poorest in fifteen years, and the U.S. Navy was preventing Japan from utilizing food sources on the Asian mainland. Industry was in critical condition, and the people still did not realize how near defeat had come. Home Minister Genki Abe feared that unconditional acceptance of the Potsdam Declaration would trigger riots and assassinations.

Mentally counting noses, Suzuki saw that a majority was in favor of peace, but the decision required unanimity. So at 4:30 he recessed the cabinet for an hour while he and Togo hurried to the Imperial Palace to brief the Emperor on the events of the day. They requested and received authority to recall the Supreme War Council for an Imperial Conference.

Then it was back to the cabinet at 6:30 P.M. for another three and a half hours of mind-numbing, repetitive discussions. Finally Suzuki adjourned the meeting and set about recalling the Supreme War Council for the Imperial Conference. It was a thoroughly miserable session. Everyone was exhausted, and the site—the Imperial air-raid shelter—was poorly air-conditioned. A summation of the discussions, which lasted until 2 A.M. on August 10, would be fruitless, because they were an instant replay of what had gone before, and no one had changed his mind. If anything, the debate was more forceful because of the presence of the Emperor. Finally Suzuki played his trump card. Amid the disbelieving gasps of his colleagues, he approached Hirohito and respectfully begged that His Imperial Majesty give his decision and that the conference accept it.

The Emperor's reply was prompt, brief, and unmistakable, although anguished: "I agree with the proposal of the Foreign Affairs Minister. . . . Heretofore, the plans of the Army and Navy authorities have always been erroneous and inopportune." Plans for the defense of the homeland had lagged; air raids were "becoming more intense day by day. I do not want to see the people continue to suffer from distress any longer. Also, I do not desire any further destruction of cultures, nor any additional misfortune for the peoples of the world. On this occasion, we have to bear the unbearable."*

There could be no further discussion; the Emperor had spoken. Suzuki carried out the remaining formality of reconvening the cabinet and secured its unanimous agreement.

* Several versions exist of Hirohito's words. We have quoted from the statement of Sumisha Ikeda, who, as chief of the General Planning Bureau, was present and apparently took copious notes.

The days immediately following dispatch of the conditional acceptance of the Potsdam Declaration must have been little short of agony for those Japanese in high places who wanted peace and wanted it promptly. In addition to the suspense of awaiting the Allied reply, the possibility had to be faced that the armed forces might revolt, stage a coup d'état, and throw the nation back into all-out war.

A government press release designed to alert the people to an impending crisis could only have added to their confusion. It ended: "We must admit our fortunes are now at their lowest ebb. . . . But at the same time, the government expects you, the one hundred million people of Japan, to overcome all difficulties to uphold our national polity." Against this ominous but vague statement, the reader could balance one from the Ministry of War exhorting the officers and men of the army "to fight doggedly to the end in this holy war for the defense of our divine land." Anami had not authorized this dispatch, but he decided it was too late to withdraw it.

Sentiment for continuing the war was widespread in the armed forces, and by no means was it confined to young hotheads. Vice Admiral Matome Ugaki (6–3), commander- in-chief of the Fifth Air Fleet, was horrified

6–3 Vice Admiral Matome Ugaki, commander-in-chief, Fifth Air Fleet.

to learn that Japan had sued for peace. He could not admit that the Navy was no longer a viable fighting force; besides, the Army had large forces available. And even when organized resistance failed, the Japanese "must continue a guerrilla warfare under the Emperor and never give up the war." Eventually the enemy would have to abandon the attempt.

The Allied reply stirred up further controversy, because it did not contain the requested guarantees regarding the Emperor. Instead, "From the moment of surrender the authority of the Emperor and the Japanese Government to rule the State shall be subject to the Supreme Commander of the Allied Powers. . . . The ultimate form of Government of Japan shall be established by the freely expressed will of the Japanese people."

To Togo, this last sentence was all the guarantee needed, for it was inconceivable that the Japanese people would not vote to continue the dynasty. Others were not so sure. Hiranuma went over to the opposition, as did Suzuki until Kido talked him out of it. Suzuki's switch was not too surprising; for months of his premiership he had urged fighting to the bitter end.

Antisurrender sentiment reached a high pitch. Even Captain Fuchida, normally a practical, clearheaded individual, was caught up in it and was helping plot a coup d'état. Then he encountered an Eta Jima naval academy classmate, Rear Admiral Prince Nobuhito Takamatsu, a brother of the Emperor. The prince assured Fuchida that his brother did indeed desire to surrender immediately to secure peace. Thereupon Fuchida agreed to try to cancel the coup.

Prince Takamatsu's assurance of the Imperial wishes was all Fuchida needed, but other recalcitrant officers refused to believe that the Emperor truly wanted to surrender. They were sure that venal politicians had forced him into this position. Others, like Ugaki, continued to urge a fight to the finish. Vice Admiral Takijiro Onishi (6–4), Toyoda's deputy chief of staff and founder of the kamikazes, cornered Toyoda and Umezu on the night of August 13, and urged them to "formulate a plan for certain victory." He argued that the Japanese "would never be defeated if we were prepared to sacrifice 20,000,000 Japanese lives in a 'special attack' effort."

Fortunately for Japan, Emperor Hirohito was just as determined to end the war as his more belligerent subjects were to continue fighting. The final decision came on the morning of August 14 at an Imperial Conference convoked, against all precedent, by Hirohito himself. Suzuki, now back on track, conducted the proceedings forcefully. Anami and Umezu again presented their view, but were much too emotional for clarity. Toyoda did better, but the Emperor was not convinced. He considered the Allied reply acceptable. He knew the results would be difficult for his armed forces to bear, but he could not endure permitting his people to suffer any

6-4 Vice Admiral Takijiro Onishi, deputy chief of staff, Imperial Japanese Navy.

longer. Struggling to maintain his composure, he asked the ministers to prepare an Imperial rescript for him to broadcast to the nation. And he offered to go anywhere to talk to the troops if so requested. As he walked slowly out, every man in the room was sobbing.

Revolt still flamed; a group of army officers invaded the palace grounds determined to find and destroy the Emperor's recording. But the attempt failed, and gradually organized resistance faded. A number of the diehards committed suicide, among them Anami, Onishi, and Ugaki.

At noon on August 15 every Japanese with access to a radio sat within range in anticipation of an announced broadcast by the Emperor himself. Whatever the subject, it must be momentous, because never before had Hirohito addressed his people directly. But very few considered that he might be about to announce surrender. At the stroke of twelve, an announcer requested all listeners to arise. A brief pause; then came the national anthem, "Kimigayo," and at last the Emperor's voice. His speech was moving and well expressed; however, it is questionable how many of his listeners took it all in, for the speechwriters had couched it in court Japanese—virtually a different language from the tongue of the people. But one fact came through loud and clear—Japan had surrendered. The nation went into something verging on total shock.

The government-controlled media had never let the public know how badly the war was going, so despite the "rain of ruin," not just from the two atomic bombs but from months of conventional bombings, the fact of surrender was traumatic. Some wept uncontrollably; others wandered about in a daze. Still others prayed at Buddhist or Shinto places of worship. At Fukuoka on Kyushu army officers dragged out sixteen American prisoners of war and chopped them into pieces with swords. Many gathered near the Imperial palace, a few raising their voices in "Kimigayo" or in cries of "Banzai!" for the Emperor, but most stood or knelt in silent grief and sympathy.

Far different were the scenes across the Pacific as the word reached the American people. Times Square in New York City erupted in a never-to-be-forgotten moment of frenzied joy (6–5). Indeed, every American city and town went into virtual hysteria, such was the relief and newfound happiness. Celebrations went on into the night, as demonstrated by these sailors and their girls riding atop an automobile in Washington, D.C. (6–6). A

6–5 V-J Day in Times Square, New York City, August 14, 1945. Americans celebrate their hard-won victory over the Japanese empire.

6-6 Every American town rejoiced at the news of the Japanese acceptance of the surrender terms.

6-7 The headlines of this Washington *Times-Herald* extra for August 15, 1945, said it all.

headline in Washington's *Times-Herald* for August 15 summed it all up (6–7).

Perfect strangers embraced in the fellowship of peace with victory (6–8). Unfortunately, some used the celebration as a cloak for criminal activities; here and there rape, looting, and even killing marred the euphoria. Many, however, found this an occasion for prayer, for solemn reflection, and for remembrance of what this victory had cost in American and other Allied blood (6–9).

Of course, the event had a special significance for members of the armed forces, particularly so for those in the Pacific theater. They would not have to invade Japan in what many expected to be the bloodiest battle of all; if they went to Japan, it would be as part of the Occupation. But above all, they would be going home. No wonder sailors on board the escort carrier *Bougainville* broke into a dance of victory (6–10). At the naval amphibious base on Manus in the Admiralty Islands, members of the 22nd Special Naval Construction Battalion posted triumphant signs: WAR IS OVER! GOODBYE PACIFIC, HELLO USA (6–11).

Times Herald

EXTRA!   WASHINGTON, D. C.   WEDNESDAY, AUGUST 15, 1945   PRICE 5¢   EXTR

TRUMAN ANNOUNCES 'WAR IS OVER'

By WILLIAM K. HUTCHINSON

The White House, Aug. 14.

The war is ended.

President Truman announced tonight that fighting in the Second World War ended when Japan accepted complete unconditional surrender.

He officially declared August 15 and 16, Wednesday and Thursday, legal holidays to permit payment of time and a half to essential workers.

6-8 A sailor enfolds a young nurse in an impromptu embrace. Many people have claimed to be the couple shown here. Although very similar to the photo by Albert Eisenstaedt appearing in the August 27, 1945, issue of *Life* magazine, this one was actually taken by a Navy photographer, one Lieutenant Jorrensen. Jorrensen stood about two steps to the right of Eisenstaedt. The sailor in whites behind the embracing pair also appears in the *Life* photo.

6-9 Women kneel and pray in St. Patrick's Cathedral on Fifth Avenue, New York City.

6-10 Sailors on board the escort carrier *Bougainville* (CVE-100) erupt into a spontaneous victory dance upon hearing the news of Japan's surrender.

6-11 The 22nd Special Naval Construction Battalion celebrates the end of the war at the naval amphibious base on Manus, Admiralty Islands.

6-12 Men on the destroyer escort *Wileman* (DE-22) voice unanimous joy that their days of cramped quarters will soon be at an end.

The crew of the destroyer escort *Wileman* received word of the surrender while at Kwajalein. One wonders whether any of the young men on board reflected on the innumerable individual sacrifices that had brought them to this day, including those of Lieutenant William Wolfe Wileman, for whom their vessel was named. He was killed during an emergency landing of his damaged F4F Wildcat on Guadalcanal following an air battle with Zeroes of the Tainan Air Group on September 13, 1942, during the dark days of the Pacific war's first year (6–12).

For no men could the day have meant more than those of the 509th Composite Group. After the dust and adrenaline of the initial celebration settled, at least a portion of the men on Tinian paused to give thanks that nearly four years of conflict had come to a merciful conclusion (6–13 and 6–14).

6-13, 6-14 On Tinian, Father Toomey celebrates Mass with the 509th Composite Group on August 16, 1945.

CHAPTER 7

Surrender!

Its work done, the Suzuki cabinet resigned en masse. The old admiral bore the brunt of the superpatriots' displeasure, and was hunted from place to place until after the Occupation began. His successor was an uncle of Hirohito's, Prince Naruhiko Higashikuni. The prince was considered to be a man of limited brainpower, but he had been smart enough to oppose vigorously engaging in war with the United States. Now that the defeat he foresaw had come about, he would play an important role as a direct representative of the throne to the government and vice versa. His foreign minister was Mamoru Shigemitsu (7–1), a seasoned diplomat who had been ambassador to the United Kingdom and the Soviet Union, as well as twice foreign minister in previous cabinets.

General of the Army Douglas MacArthur had been selected as Supreme Allied Commander and would head the Occupation forces. He lost no time in making his wishes known. One of his first demands was for a delegation to fly to Manila for a dual purpose: to turn over all information about the current Japanese military and to receive the Allied Occupation plans. Naturally there were no volunteers for this highly distasteful mission. Umezu, who as chief of staff was the obvious choice as leader of the delegation, flatly refused to go. His deputy, Lieutenant General Torashiro Kawabe, was drafted in Umezu's place.

Elaborate security measures surrounded the flight to Manila. The mission had nothing to fear from the Americans, but plenty to fear from hotheaded Japanese bitterly opposed to the surrender. So when the delegation left Haneda on August 19, they flew across Tokyo Bay to Kisarazu Air Base. There they had lunch, prepared by specially picked cooks, as a precaution against poison. Then they transferred to two battered Mitsubishi "Betty"

7-1 Foreign Minister Mamoru Shigemitsu.

bombers, painted white with large green crosses in accordance with MacArthur's instructions. They flew due south for about 110 miles, then turned west toward the Ryukyus. An escort of a U.S. aircraft accompanied them to Ie Shima, where the delegation transferred to a U.S. C-54 for the final leg to Manila.

Lieutenant Geneneral Richard K. Sutherland, MacArthur's chief of staff, conducted the proceedings. One item worried the Japanese exceedingly. The initial plan called for the Americans to land at Atsugi Air Base on

August 23. A revolt at Atsugi had just been put down, but pockets of rebellion remained and the army had not yet been disarmed. Four days was much too soon for a safe arrival. Kawabe therefore asked for a delay of ten days. At first Sutherland ignored the request, but at the end of the session did agree to an additional five days, moving the date back to August 28.

Most of the proceedings, however heart-rending to the Japanese, could be charged to the fortunes of war. But at the last minute, a situation arose that appeared to be a calculated insult. Washington had prepared the draft of a surrender proclamation to be issued in the Emperor's name. Instead of the formal Imperial pronouns, the document used the common ones. This was probably due to ignorance rather than malice, and fortunately someone on the American team caught the errors. Quickly the Allied Translation and Interpreter Section prepared a corrected version. Colonel Sidney Mashbir, who spoke fluent Japanese and had served as interpreter, conveyed the apologies of Major General Charles A. Willoughby, MacArthur's intelligence chief. This courtesy pleased and surprised the Japanese who departed Manila feeling considerably more satisfied.

Instructions to cease all air operations reached Admiral William F. Halsey's Third Fleet at 5:40 A.M. on August 15. Two missions were already airborne, and Vice Admiral John S. McCain, commander, Task Force 38 (7–2), immediately recalled them. One jettisoned its bombs into the sea and returned safely. The other had reached Japan when the pilot received the word, and fifteen or twenty Japanese planes pounced on the six Hell-

cats over Tokurozama airfield. The Americans shot down nine Japanese, but lost four in the process.

Later that morning Admiral Nimitz directed the Navy to "cease all offensive operations against Japan." At Halsey's direction, his flagship, *Missouri,* sounded her whistle and siren for a full minute at 11:00 A.M., while the crew broke his personal flag and the battle colors at the foremast and mainmast. While this celebration was in progress, several Japanese planes, whose pilots had not received a cease-fire order, neared Task Force 38, bent on battle. In short order all were shot down or driven away.

The fighting might be over officially, but the Allies took nothing on faith. Their navies kept on the alert until after the actual signing of the surrender on September 2. *Missouri* had been selected as the site of that ceremony. No one could have looked forward to the event more eagerly than Halsey, who hated the Japanese bitterly and personally.

As little was known regarding Tokyo Bay, it was imperative to utilize Japanese harbor pilots experienced in navigating through obstructions, minefields, and so on. Arrangements were made for a Japanese destroyer to bring these pilots to *Missouri* via the U.S. destroyer *Nicholas,* then take to Yokosuka Naval Base the U.S. party authorized to take over that site. The Japanese destroyer *Hatsuzakura* appeared on the horizon at 7:10 A.M. on August 27 (7–3). All hands on the U.S. ships went to battle stations to guard against "possible enemy treachery." Just what harm *Hatsuzakura* could have done is questionable, because, as instructed, her crew

7-2 Vice Admiral John S. McCain, commanding Task Force 38, comes on board *Missouri* (BB-63) via boatswain's chair for a conference with Admiral William F. Halsey, Commander, Third Fleet, on August 15, 1945.

7-3 Her naval ensign fluttering from the mainmast, the Japanese destroyer *Hatsuzakura* steams alongside USS *Nicholas* (DD-449) on August 27, 1945, before the transfer of naval officers and harbor pilots to *Missouri* for discussions regarding entry of the Third Fleet into Tokyo Bay.

had lowered her guns, opened their breeches, and emptied the torpedo tubes, while only enough personnel to man a small boat were on deck. But Halsey trusted no Japanese any further than he could have thrown the Washington Monument, so he took no chances during the transfer. He kept *Missouri*'s entire secondary battery trained on the forlorn relic throughout the transfer.

At 7:23, *Nicholas* closed on *Hatsuzakura* and her whaleboat came aboard the Japanese destroyer to receive the transfer party (7–4). There two U.S. officers examined a sword the delegation had brought along (7–5). In turn *Nicholas* closed on *Missouri* at 8:47 and the Japanese party clambered aboard (7–6). It comprised Captain Takasaki of the Yokosuka District Naval Station, Captain Inao Otani from Naval Headquarters, harbor pilot Commander Furatani, and an interpreter. The latter was a young ensign who spoke cultured English; and Halsey's own interpreter, Commander Gilven M. Slonin, hazarded a guess that he may have been a member of the Imperial

7-4 *Nicholas*'s whaleboat comes aboard *Hatsuzakura* to take on board the Tokyo Bay emissaries.

7-5 On board *Nicholas,* the Japanese harbor delegation offers a sword for examination by two American naval officers.

family, because he was "curt and condescending" to the two captains, though they were his seniors in naval rank.

This quartet was on board *Missouri* by 8:55. Later in the morning, the destroyer *Stockholm* (DD-683) came alongside and exchanged pilots, trading Lieutenant Commander Kato for Furatani. Many aboard *Missouri* watched the arrival of the Japanese with interest. Surveying the entire operation on *Missouri*'s signal bridge was Chaplain Paul L. O'Connor, a recent addition to the ship's complement. He described the scene in a letter to a friend written on August 31: "A small Jap destroyer, carrying emissaries and a pilot, was off our starboard quarter. All our 5 inch guns were bearing directly on it. The Japs transferred over to one of our destroyers [*Nicholas*] then swung aboard *Missouri.*"

As O'Connor cast a wary eye upon the foe, he felt someone brush him aside; it was none other than Halsey. The chaplain's assessment of his fleet commander is worth noting, because it contrasts sharply with the popular view of the admiral, who was by now almost a mythic figure to press and public:

> There is a bustle behind me and Halsey pushes his way alongside of me. He looks older than his pictures, face more lined, eye-brows more bushy; he offsets a long peaked cap and he has an evil, yellow-tooth grin. He is also most profane. I can see why no one out here thinks much of him. His first words were "Are they giving those sons-of-bitches life jackets? If they fall in let the bastards drown!"

Motion picture photographers were active, and Halsey did not disappoint them. O'Connor watched with cool amusement as the camera swung on Halsey: "He gestures and pretends he's speaking, then strikes the fight-

7-6 Encumbered by chart cases, Commander Furatani clambers on board *Missouri* at 8:55, "welcomed" by a lieutenant (right) and a member of the ship's Marine detachment (left).

ing mariner pose, feet wide apart, jaw set, steely eyes gazing into the distance. I hope the pictures come out well. He tried so awfully hard."

During the session, Halsey's chief of staff, Rear Admiral Robert B. Carney, received detailed hydrographic information and charts of the mine fields, while the Japanese were given specific instructions regarding the occupation of Yokosuka Naval Base, of which Carney was to take control at 10:30 in the morning of August 30 (7–7).

With the aid of the harbor pilots, *Missouri* entered the Sagami Sea, anchoring at 1:27 P.M. on August 27 on 25 fathoms. At a distance lay two British battleships, *Duke of York* and *King George V.* The former flew the flag of Admiral Sir Bruce Fraser, designated to sign for the United Kingdom at the upcoming surrender ceremony (7–8).

Early in the morning of August 29, *Missouri* weighed anchor, getting under way from the Sagami Sea at 4:56. By 9:25, she had dropped anchor in Berth F71, Tokyo Bay, where she would await the final surrender. Halsey later averred that his "life reached its climax" at that moment of anchoring in Tokyo Bay.

At two in the afternoon, he left *Missouri* to visit Fleet Admiral Chester Nimitz in *South Dakota* (7–9). As it turned out, Halsey actually welcomed Nimitz on board,

7-7 Halsey's chief of staff, Rear Admiral Robert B. Carney (at left, wearing a baseball cap) goes over charts of the Sagami Sea and Tokyo Bay with Captain Takasaki, Captain Otani, and the interpreter. The Missouri state seal is at left. Note the sweat-soaked American officer with binoculars at center.

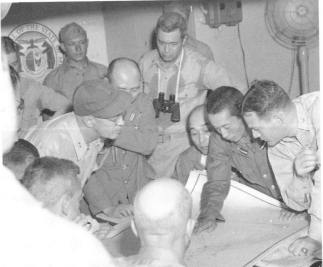

7-8 August 27, 1945, 6:16 P.M. Sunset over Fujiyama, seen from *Missouri*'s bridge as she lay at anchor on the evening of her arrival in the Sagami Sea. Other vessels lie in the distance, including (at center) two Royal Navy battleships, *Duke of York* and *King George V.*

7-9 Halsey welcomes Fleet Admiral Chester W. Nimitz on board the USS *South Dakota* (BB-57) in Tokyo Bay, August 29, 1945. The purpose of the visit was to discuss early recovery of Americans from the prisoner-of-war camps around Tokyo.

the latter having only just arrived in the area via seaplane. Halsey needed Nimitz's help. MacArthur had directed that no recovery of prisoners of war be undertaken until the Army was ready to participate. However, two British prisoners, picked up from a beach, told a tale "of such inhumanity" that Halsey and his staff found it difficult to credit until a Red Cross representative corroborated it the next day. Therefore Halsey believed, and Nimitz agreed, that the desperate situation in the various camps near Tokyo warranted immediate attention. Accordingly, Nimitz authorized Halsey to send a task group, which included the hospital ship *Benevolence* (AH-12), to proceed to Tokyo and commence rescue operations. At 3:43 that afternoon Halsey returned to *Missouri* to make arrangements. By nightfall, 800 prisoners had been delivered from captivity.

By August 30, a survivor of Pearl Harbor, the battleship *West Virginia,* had joined *Missouri* in Tokyo Bay to await the Japanese surrender (7–10 and 7–11).

Meanwhile, Atsugi airfield, where MacArthur would land, was being readied. Substantial disagreement exists

regarding the identity of the first U.S. aviator to land in Japan. Halsey relayed the claim that a "brash young pilot" from *Yorktown* (CV-18), had landed at Atsugi on August 27, "wholly against orders," and had made the Japanese paint a sign reading "Welcome to the U.S. Army from the Third Fleet." Others give credit to two Army Air Forces P-38 pilots who claimed to have run out of gas.

In any case, the first official American party to reach Atsugi was an advance force of some 150 men under Colonel C. T. Tench. Tench had rather expected that his first step onto Japanese soil would be his last, but after some initial nervousness on both sides he was reasonably satisfied that MacArthur could land safely and begin the business of occupation.

Soon other units began to arrive (7–12 and 7–13). The 11th Airborne Division landed at Atsugi early on the thirtieth. The division band was playing when MacArthur arrived at 2:19 that afternoon, sporting his corncob pipe and shirt open at the neck (7–14). Lieutenant General Robert L. Eichelberger, commanding

7-10 Flying Halsey's four-star flag, *Missouri* lies at anchor in Tokyo Bay on August 30, 1945.

7-11 Pearl Harbor survivor USS *West Virginia* (BB-48) rests in Tokyo Bay after arriving on August 30.

7-12 U.S. naval officers and their interpreter pose in front of a Japanese J1N1-R "Irving" fighter after landing the first U.S. combat aircraft at Atsugi airfield near Tokyo on August 29, 1945. Those present are (l-r): Lieutenant Commander Don Thorburn, Lieutenant Commander E. V. Wedell, interpreter Toda, Lieutenant Commander John N. MacInnes, Lieutenant W. V. Ballew, and Lieutenant Commander Cliff McDowell.

7-13 Naval officers with members of the Soviet legation of Atsugi (l-r): Lieutenant Commander MacInnes, Lieutenant Commander Thorburn, Mr. Samiloff of the Soviet legation, Lieutenant W. V. Ballew, Commander Anatoly Rodinov of the Soviet Navy, and Lieutenant Commander Wedell.

7-14 General of the Army Douglas MacArthur talks with Allied and Japanese newsmen upon his arrival at Atsugi airfield on August 30, 1945.

general of the Eighth Army, personally greeted him. Throughout the war, MacArthur's top officers, although not the general himself, had worn sidearms. Today, however, they were unarmed. According to MacArthur's aide, Colonel Sid Huff, the general was sure that, the Emperor having spoken, his subjects would obey; hence there was no danger. With Eichelberger and staffs in tow, MacArthur set off for Yokohama, some twenty miles distant. The procession was not exactly an impressive one, consisting of a number of old cars, some of them charcoal burners; and several breakdowns slowed progress. Finally reaching Yokohama, MacArthur set up his headquarters. There, he and his staff made final arrangements for the surrender.

The Japanese had experienced some little trouble in selecting the top members of the eleven-member surrender delegation. Premier Prince Higashikuni was obviously out: The Imperial family could not be personally involved. His deputy, Prince Konoye, sidestepped the assignment. So it fell to Mamoru Shigemitsu to head the civilian contingent. He had long hoped for peace, and could accept the present humiliation as the preamble to a peaceful future. The task of representing the Supreme Command fell to General Umezu, that incorrigible diehard. At first he threatened to commit suicide if selected, but the Emperor personally talked him into participation.

Four American destroyers ferried the various players in the surrender drama from the Customs House Pier at Yokohama to their rendezvous aboard *Missouri.* Carrying the Japanese delegation (7–15), *Lansdowne* cast off at seven A.M. from alongside *Nicholas,* which would shortly depart Yokohama with a contingent of American and Allied dignitaries. *Buchanan* (DD-484) would ferry MacArthur, his staff, and others. *Taylor* (DD-468) drew the less glamorous assignment of transporting the press corps and its retinue of correspondents and photographers.

At 7:26 the crew of *Buchanan* piped MacArthur and his staff on board (7–16). Among the generals was Major General Curtis E. LeMay. Originally, Nimitz had designated a landing craft, considerably done up, to transport MacArthur. After viewing the "general's barge," the Supreme Allied Commander announced that he had no intention of riding twenty miles in such a craft. He huffed, "I want a destroyer, and I want a new destroyer!" Nimitz gave him *Buchanan*—not exactly new, but an appropriate mount.

Admiral Sir Bruce Fraser, representing the United Kingdom, had only a short distance to travel from aboard *Duke of York* (7–17).

Earlier in the morning, at 7:07, *Missouri* had embarked members of the press, giving the reporters and photographers almost two hours to jockey for position. By 7:50, the battleship's crew was in place. At 8:03, *Nicholas* arrived alongside and disembarked the majority of the Allied dignitaries. Nimitz came on board from *South Dakota* at 8:05, and *Missouri* broke out his five-star flag.

During the brief wait, General Joseph W. Stilwell of China fame chatted with fellow officers (7–18). The day was cloudy, but Fujiyama's symmetrical shape was visi-

7-15 Members of the Japanese delegation board USS *Lansdowne* (DD-486) at 6:33 A.M. on September 2, 1945, for the 1-hour-45-minute voyage to *Missouri.*

7-16 An honor guard presents arms at Yokohama as MacArthur arrives for the voyage to surrender site. *Buchanan* lies moored at right.

7-18 General Joseph W. Stilwell (left) talks to a group of American officers while awaiting the surrender ceremony.

7-17 Admiral Sir Bruce Fraser, the United Kingdom's signatory to the surrender, steps onto *Missouri* after the short hop from *Duke of York*.

7-19 *Missouri*'s graceful bow frames Mount Fuji. Note anchor chain and Union Jack. Either *Duke of York* or *King George V* lies in the distance at left.

7-20 The scene on *Missouri* just moments before the surrender ceremony.

ble in the distance (7–19). In those interim moments, *Missouri* was indeed an imposing sight (7- 20), her crew in spotless whites (7–21), her scout planes on her catapults (7–22).

Buchanan pulled alongside *Missouri* at 8:38 with MacArthur's party. The general boarded the battleship five minutes later, and his personal flag broke out alongside Nimitz's (7–23 and 7–24).

7-21 Her crew mustered in dress whites, *Missouri* stands ready to receive the Japanese delegation on the morning of September 2, 1945. Note the *Gleaves*-class destroyer (likely *Buchanan*) standing by on her starboard beam.

7-22 *Missouri* from astern. Note the Curtiss SC-1 Seahawk scout planes on her catapults.

7-23, 7-24 Accompanied by Nimitz, MacArthur strides by the barbette of Number 2 turret toward the cloth-bedecked mess table, on which lies the Instrument of Surrender.

Shortly thereafter the Japanese delegation climbed aboard. For Shigemitsu this was no less physically than psychologically painful. He had lost a leg to a bomb thrown in China, and his artificial limb never fit properly, so any unusual pressure on the stump was agonizing (7–25). He brought proper credentials (7–26 and 7–27), but nobody seemed interested in receiving them.

In their stiff uniforms and formal morning dress, the Japanese contrasted sharply with the Americans, whose attire consisted predominantly of khakis, with open-necked shirts. Members of the Japanese delegation stood expressionless during the proceedings, which remained almost deathly quiet. In photo 7–28, however, Toshikazu Kase glanced right, sizing up the American officers. Kase wrote later that millions of eyes seemed to be bearing down on him. Colonel Ichiji Sugita noted the many sailors who had seated themselves on the barrels of *Missouri*'s 16-inch guns—an informality the Japanese navy never would have permitted.

At 9:02, MacArthur took his place before the microphone and opened the proceedings with a brief but eloquent address (7–29). Kase, who was fluent in English, caught every word and nuance, and later expressed himself as "thrilled beyond words, spellbound, thunderstruck." Whatever he had expected, it was not this solemn but fervent plea for victors and vanquished to work together to build a better world.

7-25 *Missouri*'s welcoming party comes to attention and salutes as Foreign Minister Shigemitsu, visible at left in the top hat, struggles to board the battleship at 8:56.

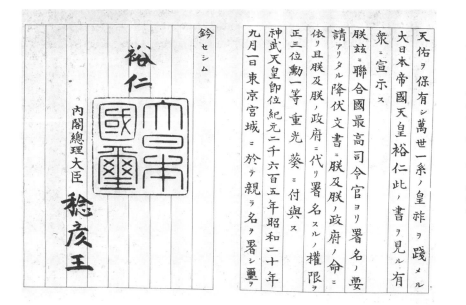

7-26, 7-27 Shigemitsu's credentials. The Japanese were not asked to present them.

HIROHITO,

By the Grace of Heaven, Emperor of Japan, seated on the Throne occupied by the same Dynasty changeless through ages eternal,

To all to whom these Presents shall come, Greeting!

We do hereby authorise Mamoru Shigemitsu, Zyosanmi, First Class of the Imperial Order of the Rising Sun to attach his signature by command and in behalf of Ourselves and Our Government unto the Instrument of Surrender which is required by the Supreme Commander for the Allied Powers to be signed.

In witness whereof, We have hereunto set Our signature and caused the Great Seal of the Empire to be affixed.

Given at Our Palace in Tōkyō, this first day of the ninth month of the twentieth year of Syōwa, being the two thousand six hundred and fifth year from the Accession of the Emperor Zinmu.

Seal of the Empire

Signed: HIROHITO.

Countersigned: Naruhiko-ō
Prime Minister

7-28 The Japanese delegation presents itself to MacArthur. In the group are (front row, l-r): Mamoru Shigemitsu, foreign minister; General Toshijiro Umezu, chief of staff; (second row, l-r) Lieutenant General Shinichi Miyazaki, director of the First Department of the army division of General Headquarters; Katsuo Okazaki, director general of the Central Liaison Office; Rear Admiral Sadatoshi Tomioka, director of the First Department of the navy division of General Headquarters; Toshikazu Kase, director of the Third Department of the Board of Information; Major General Yatsuji Nagai, army staff officer of General Headquarters; (third row l-r) hidden, Rear Admiral Ichiro Yokoyama, navy ministry; hidden, Saburo Ohta, director of the Third Department of the Central Liaison Office; Captain Katsuo Shiba, navy staff officer of General Headquarters; Colonel Ichiji Sugita, army staff officer of General Headquarters. Lieutenant C. F. Wheeler took this and many U.S. Navy photographs from this vantage point.

7-29 At 9:02 A.M., MacArthur, representing all the Allied nations, steps to the microphone and addresses the gathering. From his perch on *Missouri*'s bridge, Navy photographer Lieutenant C. A. Poots preserved for posterity the entire ceremony, creating a unique record of one of history's truly memorable events.

7-30 At 9:04 A.M., the Japanese are invited to sign the Instrument of Surrender. Confused as to where to sign, Shigemitsu fumbles for his fountain pen, while Kase points out the correct place on the English copy. The delegation appears somewhat more relaxed. Saburo Ohta in his white suit, hidden in 7-28, stands at left on the third row, hat in hand. Note the scaffolding at right, built for the military and press photographers.

At precisely 9:04, the Japanese were invited to sign the Instrument of Surrender, of which there were two copies, one each in English and Japanese (7–30). Although Kase pointed out the correct place on the English copy, Shigemitsu seemed confused as to where to sign, and he had trouble with his pen. Halsey, never one to give the Japanese the benefit of the doubt, thought he was stalling. MacArthur instructed Sutherland to prompt

Shigemitsu, who thereupon signed (7–31), followed by Umezu (7–32).

Then it was the Allies' turn. MacArthur invited Lieutenant Generals Jonathan Wainwright and Sir John Percival, who, respectively, had surrendered the Philippines and Singapore to the Japanese, to stand behind him as he affixed his signature to the documents on behalf of all the Allied nations (7–33). How many Pearl Harbor sur-

7-31 Stooped over the table despite the discomfort of his artificial leg, Shigemitsu signs the Japanese copy of the surrender.

7-32 At 9:06, General Umezu signs for Imperial General Headquarters.

7-33 At 9:08, MacArthur signs for all the Allied nations while a solemn assembly of officers looks on.

vivors made it through the long war to the place of honor beside *Missouri*'s Number 2 turret is uncertain. One notable personality was present, however: Captain Edwin T. Layton, who had been the Pacific Fleet's Intelligence Officer on December 7, 1941.

Next, Nimitz signed for the United States, flanked by Halsey and Rear Admiral Forrest P. Sherman, Nimitz's deputy chief of staff (7–34).

One by one the Allied representatives affixed their signatures—General Hsu Yung-chang of China (7–35), Admiral Sir Bruce Fraser of the United Kingdom (7–36), Lieutenant General Kuzma Nikolaivich Derevyenko of the U.S.S.R. (7–37), General Sir Thomas Blamey for Australia (7–38), Colonel L. Moore Cosgrave for Canada (7–39), General Jacques LeClerc for France (7–40), Admiral Conrad Helfrich for the Netherlands,

7-35 At 9:13, General Hsu Yung-chang signs for China.

7-36 At 9:14, Admiral Sir Bruce Fraser signs for the United Kingdom.

7-37 At 9:16, Lieutenant General Kuzma Nikolaivich Derevyenko signs for the Union of Soviet Socialist Republics.

7-38 At 9:17, General Sir Thomas Blamey signs for Australia.

7-39 At 9:18, Colonel L. Moore Cosgrave signs for Canada. As Cosgrave signed the Japanese copy, he inadvertently skipped one space, displacing the last four signatures—an error the Japanese caught at the last minute.

7-40 At 9:20, General Jacques Leclerc signs for France.

and Air Vice Marshal Sir L. M. Isitt for New Zealand (7–41). Kase found himself wondering how the Japanese could ever have had the temerity to take on so many powerful nations. They must have been "fired by sheer madness."

After MacArthur closed the proceedings at 9:25, the Japanese retrieved their copy of the Instrument of Surrender and noticed that Cosgrave had signed one space down from his proper slot, moving the last four signatures down one space. The Japanese explained excitedly that their copy was not valid. MacArthur ordered Sutherland tersely, "Change the thing." According to a *New York Times* reporter, Sutherland lined through the printed names above the signatures and wrote them in below. Now satisfied, the Japanese delegation turned away (7–42).

Just as the proceedings on *Missouri* drew to a close, the sun broke from behind the overcast, spilling its light onto the ships. Simultaneously, a flight of several hundred Navy aircraft and Army B-29s swept over Tokyo Bay and the units of the fleet (7–43). *Missouri* also unfurled a flag with considerable historical significance: the Stars and Stripes that had flown over the U.S. Capitol on December 7, 1941. It had been flown three times before to signify victory—at Casablanca, at Rome, and at Berlin.

7-41 At 9:21, Admiral Conrad Helfrich signs for the Netherlands. Last to sign was Air Vice Marshal Sir L. M. Isitt for New Zealand.

7-42 A nervous footnote to the ceremony. As Shigemitsu and Kase look on, Sutherland corrects the Japanese copy of the surrender, marred by the Canadian signatory's error.

7-43 American aircraft appear over *Missouri* following the surrender ceremony. Note the victory tally on the bridge and the thirty-star flag, the same banner raised by Commodore Perry at Tokyo on July 14, 1853. It was too fragile to fly, so was displayed on the bulkhead.

7-44 Naval aircraft fly over *Missouri* after the surrender. Note the destroyers standing by to take off the press and dignitaries.

7-45 Aircraft over *Ancon* (AGC-4), hardy veteran of amphibious operations off Morocco, Sicily, Normandy, and Okinawa.

Destroyers were standing by to take off the dignitaries and press (7–44 and 7–45), the latter to leave by the destroyer *Taylor.* The Japanese received formal honors (7–46), then departed as they had arrived, by *Lansdowne* (7–47). She got under way at 9:44 A.M. Aboard the destroyer, Kase listened to MacArthur's broadcast to the States, and again was impressed and hopeful for the future. He hurriedly jotted down his impressions for Shigemitsu to take to the Emperor. At 10:32, the party disembarked at Yokohama.

MacArthur left *Missouri* at 9:58 (7–48). The other Allied representatives followed at 10:05. Last to leave was Nimitz, at 10:44. *Missouri*'s crew returned to quarters at 10:52, bringing the surrender observance to a close. This battleship had established her place in her country's history (7–49), and barring unforeseen calamity need never fear being scrapped.

7-46 The Japanese delegation receives honors as it leaves *Missouri* at the conclusion of the surrender ceremony shortly before 9:30.

7-47 Japanese on *Lansdowne* return to Yokohama. Note Saburo Ohta in his white suit, at center.

7-48 MacArthur departs *Missouri* at 9:58.

U.S.S. MISSOURI

OVER THIS SPOT ON 2 SEPTEMBER 1945 THE INSTRUMENT OF FORMAL SURRENDER OF JAPAN TO THE ALLIED POWERS WAS SIGNED THUS BRINGING TO A CLOSE THE SECOND WORLD WAR

————

THE SHIP AT THAT TIME WAS AT ANCHOR IN TOKYO BAY

LATITUDE 35° 21' 17" NORTH ~ LONGITUDE 139° 45' 36" EAST

7-49 Plaque affixed over the surrender site on the deck of *Missouri* in October 1945.

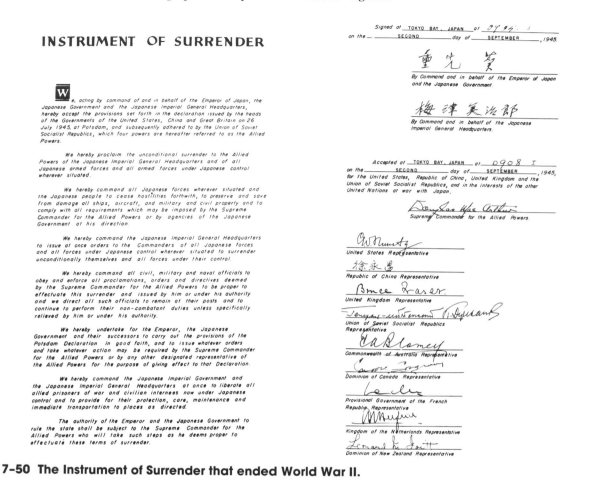

7-50 The Instrument of Surrender that ended World War II.

The Instrument of Surrender (7–50) was hand-carried to Washington for presentation to President Truman at a ceremony attended by many of those who had served him and their country well in the long years of war, and richly deserved to be present at the last scene (7–51).

7-51 Colonel Bernard Thielen presents the Instrument of Surrender to President Truman after escorting the document during its long flight from Japan. Also present are (l-r): Secretary of the Navy James Forrestal, Secretary of War Henry Stimson, General George C. Marshall, Fleet Admiral Ernest J. King, Acting Secretary of State Dean Acheson, General A. A. Vandegrift, USMC, Fleet Admiral William D. Leahy, and Lieutenant General Ira C. Eaker

CHAPTER 8

Aftermath

Japan awaited the Occupation in a state verging on panic. Lurid rumors flourished: Looting would be widespread, so Japan could expect to lose national treasures and families their cherished possessions. Women and girls could expect to be raped. This fear was so pervasive that families were urged to send their womenfolk to remote locations in the mountains. Any woman who had to remain in a city should dress as unobtrusively as possible and stay indoors; if she had to go out, she should not speak to any American male who crossed her path. All men would be killed. Particular fear was felt of reprisals against former Japanese military officers. Those portions of Tokyo that had survived the bombings would be razed. Occupation forces would commandeer all food and the Japanese, already on short rations, would starve. This had been Japanese policy in territory they occupied.

The native population was expected to feed the occupiers, and feed them well. The natives could have what was left, and if it wasn't enough, too bad!

Gradually Japanese fears lifted. There were a few early instances of rape, but MacArthur cracked down sharply, reaffirming the death penalty for that crime. Looting and destruction of property were discouraged, with private homes and national shrines placed off limits. And far from living off the land, the Occupation imported its own food supplies and even helped feed the local needy, to the surprise and gratification of the Japanese. As for the men, wholesale slaughter was not on the agenda. As the Potsdam Proclamation had promised, they were to become part of the economy. This would not be easy, but the chance was there (8–1). Ex-officers had a particular difficulty in establishing

8-1 Japanese soldiers returning to their Tokyo homes, pushing a cart loaded with their gear, passing one of the hundreds of demolished areas in the city.

8-2 Lieutenant General Tomoyuki Yamashita (left center wearing dark coat and white shirt) is arraigned before the War Crimes Commission in Manila. The members of this tribunal are (l-r):

Brigadier General E. F. Bullens, Major General C. L. Sturdevant, Major General Russell B. Reynolds, Major General J. A. Lester, and Brigadier General W. G. Walker.

themselves, because the very public service positions for which they were best qualified were denied them.

The only Japanese whose lives were at risk at Allied hands were those whom the Allies had cause to consider war criminals as opposed to honorably defeated foes. These trials began early and lasted for several years. Some were held in Japan, others near the locations involved. Thus the trial of Lieutenant General Tomoyuki Yamashita, the "Tiger of Malaya," was held at Manila, beginning on October 29, 1945 (8–2). As part of that same trial, Señorita Helena Rodriguez showed burns she received while escaping from a fire the Japanese set at the entrance to an air-raid shelter on the grounds of the German Club. Many were killed there, either in the fire or by grenades the Japanese hurled into the shelter. Señorita Rodriguez lost her mother and four brothers (8–3).

Eventually the Japanese came to realize that they could have been much worse off. Direct military government was not instituted; while subject to the Occupation, the Japanese government functioned, thus saving face and going through the motions until the inevitable day came when the Occupation was over and Japan was on her own again. Tokyo had not been split in two; she was badly damaged but whole. And despite pressure, mainly from the Russians and Australians but also some Americans, the Emperor had neither been deposed nor arraigned as a war criminal.

Children proved to be excellent icebreakers (8–4). Trotting to their homes with fists full of goodies handed out by GIs, they were proof that the average American soldier bore little resemblance to the monster rumor had painted.

The Japanese had enough real problems without fretting over imaginary ones. Victims of the atomic bombs

8-3 Helena Rodriguez testifies concerning a Japanese atrocity. Prosecuting attorney is Captain Delmas Wamege.

had a special place in the national consciousness (8–5). The freakish aspects of some wounds were especially horrifying. In photo 8–6, the patient's skin is burned in a pattern corresponding to the dark portion of the kimono she wore at the time of the explosion.

The number of blast victims far exceeded the available hospital space, and any building large and sound enough was pressed into service as a makeshift hospital. This included Kango Ginku, a Hiroshima bank. There patients rested on tatami while awaiting attention (8–7 and 8–8).

8-4 Children orphaned in the bombings of Kumamoto pose with a nurse.

8-5 Two women and a small child attend a Shinto memorial service held in the bank building for the blast victims.

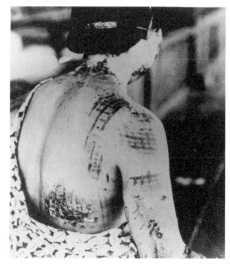

8-6 An atomic bomb survivor awaits treatment at a temporary hospital.

8-7 Blast victims rest on straw mats in a Hiroshima bank, Kango Ginku. Navy lieutenant Wayne Miller took this and the following three photos.

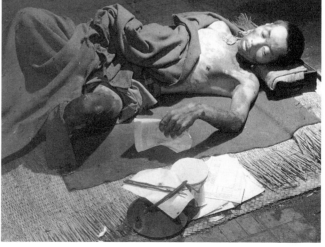

8-8 A man rests while reading in the bank building. Note the bowl and chopsticks beside his mat.

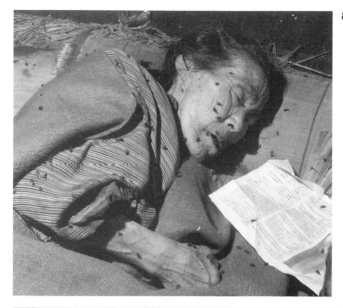

8-9 Flies cover everything in the makeshift hospital.

Sanitary provisions were primitive, to say the least (8–9). The main railway station accomodated many (8–10). Although Hiroshima's Red Cross Hospital survived the blast, the building sustained considerable damage. Burn patients overwhelmed the beleaguered staff (8–11). Facilities and resources were so limited that many patients had to be treated outside the building (8–12).

In addition to the disfigurement associated with burns, many victims suffered from keloid scars, the result of an excessive growth of fibrous tissue. The incidence of keloid formation peaked during 1946–47. Such scars are

8-10 A number of bombing victims—mostly soldiers—occupy Hiroshima's main train station.

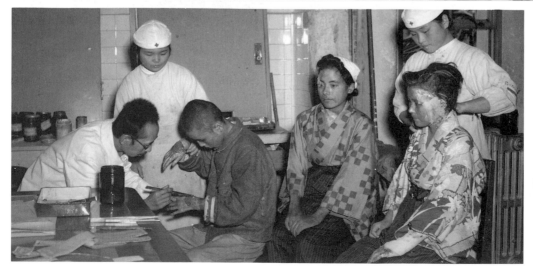

8-11 Two nurses and a doctor treat less seriously burned individuals in Hiroshima's Red Cross Hospital.

visible on the neck and cheek of the patient in photo
8–13. Others suffered pigmentation disorders resulting
from flash burns (8–14). Those with burns on or near
their joints found recovery particularly difficult. The hy-
pertropic scarring and associated contracture made full
use of the affected limbs awkward and painful (8–15).
Many patients underwent extensive skin grafts to regen-
erate large areas of flesh destroyed by burns, but these
measures were not always successful, as in the case of
the unfortunate woman shown in photo 8–16. Such ail-
ments as traumatic cataracts and leukemia appeared
around 1947, the latter reaching its climax in the period

8-12 Many patients at the Red Cross Hospital had to be treated outside.

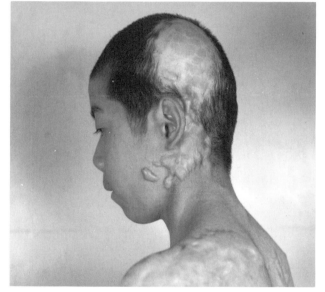

8-13 A young man from Nagasaki exhibits scars typical of many burn victims.

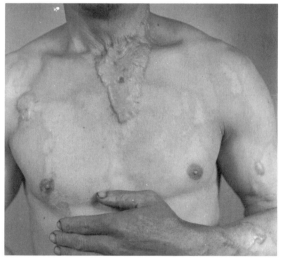

8-14 Note that while this man's clothing protected him in part, his shirt, open at the neck, exposed him to burns which resulted in the keloid on his chest.

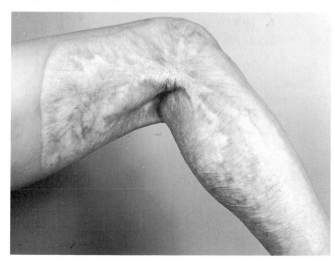

8-15 The road to recovery was difficult for the many victims who suffered serious burns around their joints.

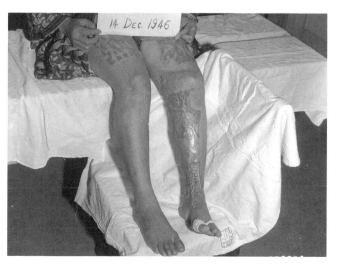

8-16 In the case of this woman, grafting was only partly successful and led to extensive scarring.

from 1950 to 1960. Following that peak, the incidence of malignant tumors increased from around 1960 and persisted for years. Deaths attributable to radiation sickness persisted for decades; an exact count is not available.

A particularly disagreeable feature of the atomic bomb soon became apparent: One need not have experienced the blast directly to become a victim. Captain Fuchida learned of this problem when, shortly after the Occupation began, he was ordered to Kure Hospital for an examination. There, to his horror, he found about fifty of his fellow officers suffering from radiation sickness. A number of them, like him, had not been in either Hiroshima or Nagasaki when the bombs exploded, but had come in the next day as investigators. The doctors put Fuchida through extensive tests, during which time two of his comrades died and the rest were obviously dying. But Fuchida was in perfect health, a fact that he considered miraculous, and who could blame him? He left the hospital badly shaken. This direct experience of the effects of *genbaku sho*—atomic bomb disease, that is, radi-

ation sickness—convinced him that however flawed and belligerent human nature might be, the atomic bomb left humanity no logical choice but peace.

The Americans were no less concerned than the Japanese with the problems the atomic bomb had raised. American medical personnel were acutely aware of the need to plan for future nuclear threats and for the type of injuries most likely to be associated with atomic explosions. The research and documentation at Hiroshima and Nagasaki unquestionably colored American thinking regarding the survivability of a nuclear war and affected American domestic and foreign policy for decades.

The United States Strategic Bombing Survey conducted extensive investigations into the results of the Hiroshima and Nagasaki bombings, as well as conventional bombings. These studies were led by Major General Orvil A. Anderson, head of the Military Analysis Division (8–17) and Rear Admiral Ralph J. Ofstie, head of

8-17 Major General Orvil A. Anderson, head of the USSBS Military Analysis Division.

8-18 Rear Admiral Ralph J. Ofstie, head of the USSBS Naval Analysis Division. Shown here as a captain in February 1944, while commanding USS *Essex* (CV-9) during strikes on Truk.

8-19 Two American Strategic Bombing Survey officers examine damage in Hiroshima. The Commercial Display Building is in the background.

the Naval Analysis Division (8–18). In photo 8–19 two USSBS officers are surveying damage in Hiroshima. They are standing south of the Commercial Display Building near the Motoyasu River, close to the radio mast visible in photo 4–13. A Navy photographer snapped a Japanese soldier walking amid Hiroshima's ruins. The only visible object that survived the blast is the tree line in the background (8–20).

In addition to documenting physical damage to Hiroshima, Strategic Bombing Survey photographers (and many others) took pictures that showed the populace attempting to carry on amid nearly total devastation. About a month after the above photo was taken, another Navy photographer portrayed some of Hiroshima's citizenry getting on with their lives. Two trolleys were back in service, and a man waited in the background (8–21).

Many Americans visiting Hiroshima and Nagasaki viewed the destruction and survivors with mixed feelings or even unmixed pity. But Australian prisoners of war traveling from the interior to begin their ocean voyage home were not likely to share such sentiments (8–22).

8–20 A Japanese soldier walking through a leveled portion of Hiroshima. Lieutenant Wayne Miller, USNR, took this picture during September 1945.

8–21 On September 26, 1945, Photographer's Mate Third Class George Almarez, USS *Appalachian* (AGC-1) snapped an attempt to return to normalcy in Hiroshima.

8–22 Australian prisoners of war en route home.

8-23 Nurses from the 308th General Hospital sleep on the ground pending construction of proper quarters.

As the Occupation progressed, Army nurses arrived in Japan to set up hospitals that would serve civilians as well as the American military population. However, finding suitable and structurally safe quarters was something of a problem at Nagasaki and Hiroshima (8–23).

Eventually, the military brought in celebrities to entertain the homesick men occupying Japan. Among them was comedian Danny Kaye, seen here in Hiroshima on October 25, 1945, after emerging from the C-47 in the background (8–24).

By December 6, 1946, Hiroshima had recovered to the point where its assistant mayor could host the Atomic Bomb Casualty Commission at luncheon (8–25).

The USSBS paid particular attention to Nagasaki as well as Hiroshima (8–26). In photo 8–27, Survey members check out a double-track railroad bridge over a small tributary of the Urakami River near ground zero, while photo 8–28 shows an American officer examining damage to the cathedral.

8-24 An Army delegation greets Danny Kaye at Hiroshima on October 25, 1945.

8-25 Members of the Atomic Bomb Casualty Commission gather for a luncheon given by the assistant mayor of Hiroshima on December 6, 1946. Kneeling (l–r) are a city official, Lieutenant F. Ullrich, Lieutenant J. Neel, Dr. Tsuzuki. Standing (l–r) are Mr. Saida, a city official, Colonel H. Johnson, Dr. R. S. Hinshaw, Dr. A. Brues, Dr. H. Volk, Dr. Matsubayashi, Lieutenant Block, Dr. Omura.

8-26 Officers from the USSBS huddle together near ground zero and examine the devastation in Nagasaki. Compare this scene with the left portion of the panorama in 5-33.

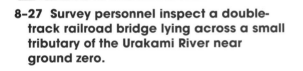

8-27 Survey personnel inspect a double-track railroad bridge lying across a small tributary of the Urakami River near ground zero.

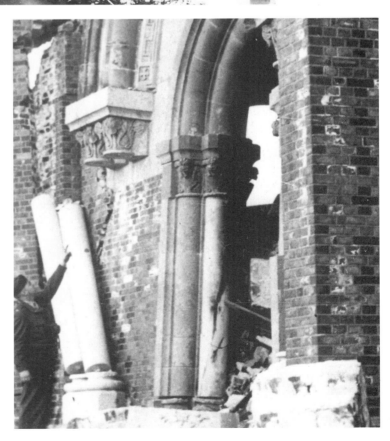

8-28 An American officer points to capitals on a wall of Urakami Cathedral from which two columns were blown away at left. Note Chinzei School on the hill beyond.

8-29 First Lieutenant D. A. McGovern of Buffalo, New York (part of the newsreel pool), prepared to take some movie footage amid the devastation of Nagasaki.

Like Hiroshima, Nagasaki attracted many visitors and curiosity-seekers outside the realm of the USSBS, as evidenced by this newsreel photographer (8–29). By spring of 1946, nature had begun to make a comeback at Nagasaki (8–30). On August 3, 1946, nearly a year after the atomic bombing, a view up the Urakami River revealed new construction in the area east of the former Mitsubishi Armament Works (8–31). Reconstruction proceeded slowly but resolutely. On May 29, 1949, the rebuilt Urakami Church was completed (8–32).

An ominous consequence of the bomb became evident within two years of the event. Sesame stalks grown in a field 300 yards from ground zero revealed an increase of 33 percent in number of seeds; but nearly 90 percent of the seeds were sterile (8–33). It would have been difficult to convince the citizens of Hiroshima and Nagasaki that they had anything for which to be grateful, but they had: If the bombs had been dropped at low altitude, the land itself would have been poisoned, and reconstruction would have been impossible, if not forever, certainly for many years.

8-30 Nagasaki, spring 1946. New shoots grow from a chestnut tree 2,000 feet from ground zero.

8-31 View looking north up the Urakami River toward Nagasaki on August 3, 1946. Note new construction in the area east of the old Mitsubishi Steel and Armament Works. The wreckage of the plant has not yet been cleared.

8-32 Slowly, a portion of the cultural infrastructure of Hiroshima and Nagasaki experienced a resurrection. Here, the rebuilt Urakami Church stands complete on May 29, 1949.

8-33 Two years after the explosion over Nagasaki, agricultural expert Takeo Furuno holds up a sesame stalk at left, grown in a field 300 yards from the hypocenter. The results presaged human genetic disorders extending out for generations.

8-34 A portion of the command crew of the 509th Composite Group after the war (l-r): Major Van Kirk, navigator; Lieutenant James W. Anderson, copilot (he actually flew in No. 91 on August 6, 1945); Major Ferebee, bombardier; Colonel Tibbets, pilot. Ferebee, looking substantially older, has shaved off his mustache.

Some of the crew members of *Enola Gay* and *Bock's Car* kept in touch after the war. Photo 8–34 shows Tibbets with a portion of the 509th Composite Group's command crew, while 8–35 pictures the atom bomb pilots and bombardiers. Nagasaki pilot Sweeney and his copilot appear in 8–36.

On July 3, 1949, *Enola Gay* was a star exhibit at the National Air Fair at Chicago's O'Hare Field. Major General Emmett J. (Rosie) O'Donnell, appearing at the right in photo 8–37, was a celebrity in his own right. As a brigadier general, he commanded the 73rd Bombardment Wing (VH), a part of LeMay's XXI Bomber Command.

On November 17, 1944, O'Donnell personally led his wing of B-29s in the first raid over Tokyo since Doolittle's strike in April 1942.

In 1952 Metro-Goldwyn-Mayer released the movie *Above and Beyond,* about Tibbets and *Enola Gay,* starring two favorites, Robert Taylor and Eleanor Parker (8–38). In contrast to the high name-recognition factor of Tibbets and *Enola Gay,* Sweeney and *Bock's Car* were virtually forgotten. To some, this may not have been totally regrettable. From the first, the dropping of the atomic bomb had been controversial; to many, *Enola Gay* and her crew carried unpleasant connotations.

8-35 The atomic bomb pilots and their bombardiers (l-r): Sweeney, Seaham, Ferebee, and Tibbets.

8-36 Nagasaki pilot and copilot after the war—Captain Charles Albury (left; promoted from first lieutenant since the mission), and Major Sweeney.

8-37 *Enola Gay* enjoys a spot on center stage at the National Air Fair at O'Hare Field in Chicago, July 3, 1949. Present (l-r) are Mr. Carl Mitman of the Smithsonian Institution; Tibbets; Ferebee; and Major General Emmett J. O'Donnell.

8-38 In the 1952 movie *Above and Beyond*, Hollywood produced a mix of wartime romance and a great story of American ingenuity and heroics. Note that Tibbets (Robert Taylor) has not yet been promoted to full colonel, an event which (in the movie) elicited a tantrum from the moody Mrs. Tibbets (Eleanor Parker).

8-39 A view looking across the Motoyasu River toward the Hiroshima Commercial Display Building.

To the Japanese, a constant reminder of the bombing was the dome of the Commercial Display Building (8–39), popularly termed the "A-Bomb Dome." Exposed to the weather, the dome's supporting framework (8–40) and masonry walls slowly crumbled away (8–41). The dome became a solemn, thought-provoking tourist attraction (8–42).

Over the years, a number of monuments to the atomic catastrophe arose close to the ground zero landmark of the A-Bomb Dome, including the Peace Bell (8–43), the Children's Peace Monument, the Memorial Monument for Hiroshima, and the Hiroshima Peace Memorial Museum. In photo 8–44 a group has gathered at the Children's Peace Monument. The figure at its top represents a girl holding an origami bird (8–45).

8-40 Exposed to the elements, the supporting framework of the dome slowly rusts away.

8-41 Likewise open to the weather, the masonry walls crumble with the passage of time.

8-42 Japanese tourists pause in front of the dome and ponder the past and future.

8-43 Just across the Motoyasu River from the A-Bomb Dome, youngsters cluster around the Peace Bell at Hiroshima.

8-44 Solemn observers gather in the rain at the Children's Peace Monument.

8-45 Atop the monolithic sculpture stands a young girl with a representation of an origami bird supported in her hands.

8-46 Eerie and surreal, the Children's Peace Monument sculptures are reminiscent of the corpses found by the thousands in the aftermath of the explosion.

The monument is known as the Tower of a Thousand Cranes because of a schoolgirl named Sadako Sasaki. Sadako, a first-year junior high school student, had contracted the "atomic disease." She believed that she would recover if she could fold 1,000 origami cranes, so every day she worked on her paper cranes. Unfortunately, the origami birds could not heal her, but one hopes they had a certain psychological value, keeping her mind and fingers busy and her spirit hopeful until her death, which came on October 25, 1955. Thereafter, Sadako's classmates started the movement toward a special memorial for the child victims of atomic bomb–induced diseases. On May 5, 1958, the project was completed. It has become customary for visitors to this touching shrine to leave an offering of paper cranes. The monument's rather surrealistic sculptures recall the charred corpses found after the explosion (8–46).

Farther south, the Memorial Monument for Hiroshima commemorates all the victims of the first atomic bomb (8–47). This monument is a popular place of pilgrimage, especially for Japanese students (8–48 and 8–49). The Hiroshima Peace Memorial Museum displays many artifacts and photographs (8–50), such as the child's jacket

8-47 Still farther south, the Memorial Monument for Hiroshima is dedicated to all victims of the first atomic bomb.

8-48 The Memorial Monument with the Commercial Display Building ruin in the background.

8-49 The Memorial Monument is a popular place for reflection, and draws many groups of Japanese students, easily identified here by their school garb.

8-50 The Hiroshima Peace Memorial Museum houses a diverse collection of artifacts and photography from the bombing's aftermath.

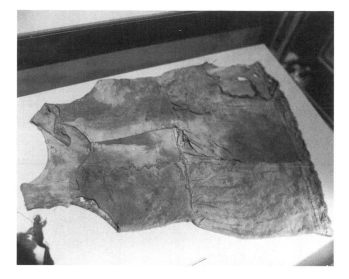

8-51 A child's jumper in the museum display.

8-52 A child's jacket shows the effect of the blast on individuals within a mile and a half of the hypocenter. Those closer in frequently had clothing burned away or blown off.

and jumper (8–51 and 8–52) and the crushed frame of a bicycle (8–53).

The older generation that experienced the bombing directly, with consequent trauma mental as well as physical, decreases year by year (8–54), but that does not mean that the memory of the event is fading. The younger generation learns about Hiroshima at a very early age (8–55 and 8–56). Perhaps naturally, the story they are taught casts Japan as an innocent victim, an interpretation that has become a part of the national psy-

che. Only very recently has Japan begun to acknowledge officially that she, too, played a not entirely sympathetic role in the Pacific war. Indeed, the atomic bomb produced at least one healthy reaction in Japan—a horror of atomic energy in all its forms, so deeply rooted that it is exceedingly unlikely she will revert to a policy of aggression in the foreseeable future.

8-53 The crushed remains of a bicycle recovered from the ruins of Hiroshima.

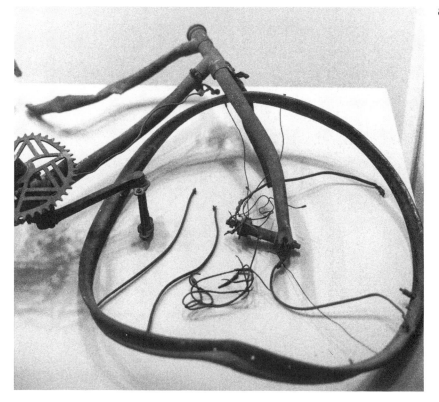

8-54 The older generation, with physical and mental scars, and firsthand memories of the A-Bomb, dwindles with every passing year.

8-55 Japanese schoolgirls at the memorial.

8-56 Younger generations have been inculcated with the history of the Hiroshima bombing from a very early age.

Chronology

October 1939	Einstein writes to Roosevelt suggesting the possibility of an atomic bomb.
November 1941	Roosevelt appoints a committee to advise him on nuclear fission.
December 7, 1941	Japan attacks the United States at Pearl Harbor.
December 1941	The Manhattan Project begins.
December 1942	A workable atomic pile is established at the University of Chicago.
September 1944	Tibbets is selected to command the 509th Composite Group.
December 17, 1944	The 509th is activated.
March 9, 1945	B-29s begin mass incendiary raids on Japan.
April 1, 1945	The battle for Okinawa begins.
April 7, 1945	The Suzuki cabinet is installed.
April 12, 1945	Roosevelt dies; Truman becomes president.
April 25, 1945	Stimson and Groves brief Truman on S-1, the atomic bomb project.
April 26, 1945	The 509th begins its move to Tinian.
May 7, 1945	Germany surrenders.
May 9, 1945	The Interim Committee on Nuclear Energy holds its first meeting.
May 31, 1945	The Interim Committee agrees to use of bomb against Japan, with no previous demonstration.
June 1945	Japan suspends work on its nuclear bomb project because of "the very critical war situation."
June 18, 1945	Truman approves the plan for invasion of Japan.
June 30, 1945	The battle for Okinawa ends.
July 16–August 2	The Big Three conference takes place at Potsdam.
July 16, 1945	The atomic bomb test at Alamogordo is successful.
July 21, 1945	First 509th operations (non-atomic) against Japan take place.
July 25, 1945	The War Department relays Truman's order to use the bomb.

July 26, 1945	Potsdam Proclamation issued. Cruiser *Indianapolis* delivers U-235 core of Little Boy to Tinian.
July 28, 1945	Japan decides to ignore the Potsdam Proclamation.
August 2, 1945	Truman gives final approval to use the bomb.
August 6, 1945	Hiroshima bomb dropped, 8:16 A.M.
August 8, 1945	The U.S.S.R. declares war on Japan.
August 9, 1945	Nagasaki bomb dropped, 10:58 A.M.
August 10, 1945	The Emperor breaks his government's deadlock, deciding on surrender, 2 A.M.
August 10, 1945	The Japanese send a message concerning terms of capitulation.
August 11, 1945	The Allies reply that the Japanese government will be subject to the Supreme Allied Commander.
August 15, 1945	The Imperial Rescript of Surrender is broadcast at noon by the Emperor's recording. V-J Day.
September 2, 1945	MacArthur accepts Japan's formal surrender aboard battleship *Missouri* in Tokyo Bay.

Selected Bibliography

Books

CHURCHILL, WINSTON S. *The Second World War,* Vol. 6: *Triumph and Tragedy.* Boston: Houghton Mifflin, 1953.

COFFEY, THOMAS M. *Imperial Tragedy.* New York: World Publishing Co., 1970.

CRAVEN, WESLEY FRANK, and JAMES LEA CATE. *The Army Air Forces in World War II,* Vol. 5, *The Pacific: Matterhorn to Nagasaki, June 1944 to August 1945.* Chicago: University of Chicago Press, 1953.

CROWTHER, J. G., and R. WHIDDINGTON. *Science at War.* New York: Philosophical Library, 1948.

DOWER, JOHN W. *Japan in War and Peace.* New York: New Press, 1993.

DUGGER, RONNIE. *Dark Star.* Cleveland: World Publishing Co., 1967.

EISENHOWER, DAVID. *Eisenhower at War 1943–1945.* New York: Random House, 1986.

Encyclopedia Americana, 1994, Vol. 19, "Atomic Bomb."

GREENFIELD, KENT ROBERTS, ED. *Command Decisions.* Washington, D.C.: Office of the Chief of Military History, Department of the Army, 1960.

HALSEY, FLEET ADMIRAL WILLIAM F., and LIEUTENANT COMMANDER. J. BRYAN III. *Admiral Halsey's Story.* New York: McGraw-Hill, 1947.

HUFF, SID, and JOE ALEX MORRIS. *My Fifteen Years with General MacArthur.* New York: Curtis, 1951.

International Encyclopedia, 1975, Vol. 2, "Radiation," and "Atomic Weapons."

KASE, TOSHIKAZU. *Journey to the* "Missouri." New Haven, Conn.: Yale University Press, 1950.

MCCULLOUGH, DAVID. *Truman.* New York: Simon and Schuster, 1992.

MORISON, SAMUEL ELIOT. *History of United States Naval Operations in World War II.* Vol. 14. *Victory in the Pacific, 1945.* Boston: Little, Brown, 1960.

MOSLEY, LEONARD. *Hirohito, Emperor of Japan.* Englewood Cliffs, N.J.: Prentice Hall, 1966.

OKUMIYA, MASATAKE, and JIRO HORIKOSHI, with MARTIN CAIDIN. *Zero! The Story of Japan's Air War in the Pacific 1941–45.* New York: Ballantine, 1957.

PRANGE, GORDON W., with DONALD M. GOLDSTEIN and KATHERINE V. DILLON. *God's Samurai: Lead Pilot at Pearl Harbor.* Washington, D.C.: Brassey's, 1990.

Reports of General MacArthur: *Japanese Operations in the Southwest Pacific Area,* Vol. 2, Part 2. Washington, D.C.: U.S. Government Printing Office, 1966.

———. Vol. 1, Supplement, 1966.

SPECTOR, RONALD H. *Eagle Against the Sun: The American War with Japan.* New York: Free Press, 1985.

SZASZ, FERENC M. *British Scientists and the Manhattan Project: The Los Alamos Years.* New York: St. Martin's Press, 1992.

TOLAND, JOHN. *The Rising Sun: The Decline and Fall of the Japanese Empire, 1936–1945.* New York: Random House, 1970.

TRUMAN, HARRY S. *Memoirs,* Vol. 1, *Year of Decision.* Garden City, N.Y.: Doubleday, 1955.

World Book, 1984, Vol. 14.

Pamphlets and Brochures

"A Brief Summary of the Atomic Bombing and Its Effects." Hiroshima Peace Memorial Museum, 1992.

"Hiroshima-Nagasaki: A Pictorial Record of the Atomic Destruction." Committee of Japanese Citizens to Send Gift Copies of a Photographic and Pictorial Record of the Atomic Bombing to Our Children and Fellow Human Beings of the World. U.S. Historical Research Center, Maxwell Air Force Base, Alabama.

"The Outline of Atomic Bomb Damage in Hiroshima." Hiroshima Peace Memorial Museum, 1978

"The Smithsonian and the *Enola Gay,*" March 15, 1994. The Air Force Association, Arlington, Va.

Articles

TIBBETS, BRIGADIER GENERAL PAUL W. "I Dropped the Atomic Bomb on Hiroshima." *Paris Match,* September 4, 1965, trans. H. D. Benington. USAF Historical Research Center, Maxwell Air Force Base, Ala.

———. "Training the 509th for Hiroshima." *Air Force Magazine,* August 1973.

Newspapers

Des Moines *Register*
The Washington Post
Air Force Times
The New York Times
Pittsburgh *Post-Gazette*

Unpublished Sources

Diary of Henry L. Stimson. New Haven, Conn.: Yale University Library.

U.S. Air Force Oral History Interview with Brigadier General Paul W. Tibbets, Jr., February 7, 1985, USAF Historical Research Center, Maxwell Air Force Base, Alabama.

Unit History, 509th Composite Group. U.S.A.F. Historical Research Center, Maxwell Air Force Base, Alabama.

General Headquarters, Far East Division, Military Intelligence Section, Historical Division, Statements of Japanese Officials on World War II, English translations:

Doc. No.

Maj. Gen. Masakazu Amano	54480	December 29, 1949
———.	59617	June 10, 1950
Lt. Gen. Seizo Arisue	52506	November 19,1949
———.	61411	August 16, 1949
General Shigeru Hasunuma	58225	March 31, 1950
Col. Saburo Hayashi	61436	December 23, 1949
V. Adm. Kenshiro Hoshina	61978	November 9, 1949
———.	53437	December 27, 1949
Sumihisa Ikeda	54479	December 23, 1949
Maj. Katsumori Kai	50732	September 15 1949
Lt. Gen. Torashiro Kawabe	50569	June 15, 1949
———.	50820	September 20, 1949
———.	45575	January 15, 1950
Marquis Koichi Kido	61541	May 17, 1949
Lt. Gen. Shinichi Miyazaki	50567	September 9, 1949
———.	50770	September 15, 1949
———.	54194	January 12, 1950
R. Adm. Katsuihei Nakamura	50565	August 20, 1950
Lt. Gen. Kanji Nishihara	54085	January 10, 1950
Dr. Yoshio Nishina	60245	May 4, 1950
———.	60246	June 29, 1950
Capt. Toshikazu Ohmae	52505	November 19, 1949
———.	53072	December 15, 1949
Lt. Col. Kiyoshi Ohta	53242	December 18, 1949
Maj. Gen. Joichiro Sanada	52336	November 12, 1949
Col. Katsuo Sato	59402	June 6, 1950
Col. Ichiji Sugita	58553	May 13, 1950
Maj. Ryoichi Tabata	50733	September 10, 1949
Lt. Col. Koji Tanaka	50575	May 5, 1949
———.	53070	December 15, 1949
Shigenori Togo	50304	May 17, 1949
Maj. Kinjiro Tokaji	50564	September 9, 1949
Admiral Soemu Toyoda	61340	September 1, 1949
Lt. Gen. Wataro Yoshinaka	50956	September 26, 1949
Maj. Gen. Yasumasa Yoshitake	50576	September 9, 1949

Photo Credits

J. Michael Wenger: 1–28, 2–8, 2–44, 4–11, 5–25

United States Army Air Forces, Smithsonian Institution, Washington, D.C.: 1–22, 4–23, 4–24, 4–25, 5–3

Smithsonian Institute, Washington, D.C.: 1–24, 1–31, 1–32, 2–2, 2–3, 2–9, 2–25, 3–14, 4–1, 4–8, 4–12, 4–13, 4–16, 4–17, 4–18, 4–31, 4–32, 4–34, 4–35, 4–36, 4–37, 4–41, 4–44, 4–45, 4–46, 4–47, 4–48, 4–49, 4–50, 4–52, 4–53, 4–54, 4–55, 4–57, 4–58, 4–59, 4–60, 4–61, 4–62, 4–63, 4–64, 4–65, 4–66, 4–68, 4–71, 4–73, 4–75, 5–10, 5–21, 5–22, 5–23, 5–26, 5–27, 5–28, 5–29, 5–30, 5–34, 5–36, 5–37, 5–38, 5–39, 5–40, 5–41, 5–42, 5–43, 5–45, 5–46, 5–48, 5–51, 5–52, 5–55, 5–56, 5–57, 5–58, 5–59, 5–60, 5–70, 5–71, 5–72, 5–73, 5–74, 5–75, 5–76, 5–77, 5–78, 5–80, 5–82, 5–83, 5–84, 5–85, 5–88, 5–89, 5–90, 5–92, 5–93, 8–17, 8–19, 8–26, 8–27, 8–29, 8–30, 8–31

Naval Historical Center, Suitland, Maryland: 1–4, 1–5, 1–34, 1–35, 2–34, 2–45, 2–46, 6–2, 6–7, 7–11, 7–14, 7–23

Air Force Historical Research Agency, Maxwell Air Force Base, Alabama: 1–23, 1–26, 1–29, 1–30, 2–1, 2–4, 2–19, 2–20, 2–21, 2–22, 2–24, 2–33, 3–1, 3–2, 3–3, 3–4, 3–5, 3–6, 3–7, 3–9, 3–11, 3–12, 3–15, 4–3, 4–6, 4–26, 4–27, 4–28, 4–29, 4–30, 5–1, 5–5, 5–6, 5–7, 5–8, 5–9, 5–20, 5–24, 6–13, 6–14, 8–34, 8–35, 8–36, 8–37, 8–38

Donald M. Goldstein and William Hendricks: 1–3, 1–6, 1–7, 1–16, 1–18, 1–19, 1–20, 1–21, 1–25, 2–18, 2–27, 3–13, 4–38, 4–40, 4–78, 6–3, 6–4, 8–1, 8–2, 8–3, 8–4, 8–39, 8–40, 8–41, 8–42, 8–43, 8–44, 8–45, 8–46, 8–47, 8–48, 8–49, 8–50, 8–51, 8–52, 8–53, 8–54, 8–55, 8–56

Robert J. Cressman: 2–41, 2–42, 2–43, 5–2, 8–18

National Archives, Washington, D.C.: 1–1, 1–2, 1–8, 1–9, 1–10, 1–11, 1–12, 1–13, 1–14, 1–15, 1–17, 1–27, 1–33, 1–36, 1–37, 2–5, 2–6, 2–7, 2–10, 2–11, 2–12, 2–13, 2–14, 2–15, 2–16, 2–17, 2–23, 2–26, 2–28, 2–29, 2–30, 2–31, 2–32, 2–35, 2–36, 2–37, 2–38, 2–39, 2–40, 2–47, 2–48, 3–8, 3–10, 3–16, 3–17, 3–18, 3–19, 3–20, 3–21, 3–22, 3–23, 3–24, 3–25, 3–26, 3–27, 3–28, 3–29, 3–30, 3–31, 4–2, 4–4, 4–5, 4–7, 4–9, 4–10, 4–14, 4–15, 4–19, 4–20, 4–21, 4–22, 4–33, 4–39, 4–42, 4–43, 4–51, 4–56, 4–67, 4–69, 4–70, 4–72, 4–74, 4–76, 4–77, 5–4, 5–11, 5–12, 5–13, 5–14, 5–15, 5–16, 5–17, 5–18, 5–19, 5–31, 5–32, 5–33, 5–35, 5–44, 5–47, 5–49, 5–50, 5–53, 5–54, 5–61, 5–62, 5–63, 5–64, 5–65, 5–66, 5–67, 5–68, 5–69, 5–79, 5–81, 5–86, 5–87, 5–91, 6–1, 6–5, 6–6, 6–8, 6–9, 6–10, 6–11, 6–12, 7–1, 7–2, 7–3, 7–4, 7–5, 7–6, 7–7, 7–8, 7–9, 7–10, 7–12, 7–13, 7–15, 7–16, 7–17, 7–18, 7–19, 7–20, 7–21, 7–22, 7–24, 7–25, 7–26, 7–27, 7–28, 7–29, 7–30, 7–31, 7–32, 7–33, 7–34, 7–35, 7–36, 7–37, 7–38, 7–39, 7–40, 7–41, 7–42, 7–43, 7–44, 7–45, 7–46, 7–47, 7–48, 7–49, 7–50, 7–51, 8–5, 8–6, 8–7, 8–8, 8–9, 8–10, 8–11, 8–12, 8–13, 8–14, 8–15, 8–16, 8–20, 8–21, 8–22, 8–23, 8–24, 8–25, 8–28, 8–32, 8–33

Index

ABOUT THE AUTHORS

DONALD M. GOLDSTEIN, Lieutenant Colonel, USAF (Ret.), is professor of public and international affairs at the University of Pittsburgh. KATHERINE V. DILLON, Chief Warrant Officer, USAF (Ret.), of Arlington, Virginia, collaborated with Dr. Goldstein and the late Dr. Gordon W. Prange on six volumes including the best-selling *At Dawn We Slept* and *Miracle at Midway,* as well as *God's Samurai: Lead Pilot at Pearl Harbor.* J. MICHAEL WENGER is a freelance historian living in Raleigh, North Carolina. He has collaborated with Dr. Goldstein and Ms. Dillon on three previous books.